ULTIMATE
JOKIEST
JOKING
JOKE BOOK
EVER WRITTEN . . . NO JOKE!

LOOKING FOR MORE JOKES TO IMPRESS
YOUR FRIENDS AND BUILD YOUR ULTIMATE
JOKEMASTER COLLECTION?

YOU'LL LOVE . . .

***THE JOKIEST JOKING JOKE BOOK
EVER WRITTEN . . . NO JOKE!***

***THE JOKIEST JOKING KNOCK-KNOCK JOKE BOOK
EVER WRITTEN . . . NO JOKE!***

***THE JOKIEST JOKING TRIVIA BOOK
EVER WRITTEN . . . NO JOKE!***

***THE JOKIEST JOKING BATHROOM JOKE BOOK
EVER WRITTEN . . . NO JOKE!***

***THE JOKIEST JOKING PUNS BOOK
EVER WRITTEN . . . NO JOKE!***

THE
ULTIMATE JOKIEST JOKING JOKE BOOK
EVER WRITTEN . . . NO JOKE!

THE HUGEST PILE OF JOKES, KNOCK-KNOCKS, PUNS, AND KNEE-SLAPPERS THAT WILL KEEP YOU LAUGHING OUT LOUD

Jokes by **Kathi Wagner,
Brian Boone,** *and* **May Roche**

Illustrations by **Amanda Brack**

CASTLE POINT BOOKS

NEW YORK

CONTENTS

INTRODUCING . . .

The funniest, silliest, most ridiculous joke book yet! *The Ultimate Jokiest Joking Joke Book Ever . . . No Joke!* is a big, fat book of our favorite jokes, knock-knocks, puns, riddles, and goofy stuff ever. Practice your best chortles, guffaws, snorts, and giggles as you laugh your way through 23 chapters of hilarity. Whether you're a fan of bathroom humor (there's a buttload of that), love some good knock-knocks (we've got you covered), enjoy some fantastic puns (there are puns of them), you'll have plenty of material for your own personal stand-up routine.

So warm up your funny bone and dive right into *The Ultimate Jokiest Joking Joke Book Ever . . . No Joke!*

1
FUNNY BONE—Zombies, Skeletons, Ghosts, etc.

What kind of story would a ghostwriter write?
A spooky one.

What do you call it when a baby vampire crawls?
A little creepy.

Why do zombies walk so slow?
Because they're dead tired.

What do mad mops do?

Kick the bucket!

How do you know if you're a ghost?
When food goes right through you.

What do baby zombies wear?
Die-pers.

What do you call zombie phones?
Dead ringers.

How do you know when two zombies are talking?
It's dead quiet.

What do little spirits like before bed?
Ghost stories.

What does a ghost say when you knock at the door?
Boo is it?

How do you know when a poltergeist is scared?
He's white as a ghost.

How did the skeleton get in the house?
It used its key.

What do you say to a zombie without a brain?
Nevermind.

How can you be sure when a zombie isn't right?
When they're dead wrong.

Why did one dog get mad at the other dog?

They had a bone to pick!

What does a ghost call its favorite person?

My Boo!

Why couldn't the stone be a grave marker?

It couldn't get a head.

What did the skeleton think of the grave?

It was a little shallow at times.

What would happen if someone took everything out of the freezer?

Ice cream.

How did the glass know everything was going to be all right?

There was a light at the end of the funnel.

Why does it take longer for a two-headed monster to answer a question?

It has to think twice.

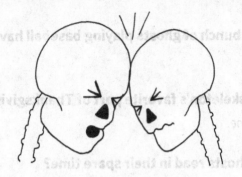

What do skeletons get
when they bump their heads?

Numbskulls!

How did the milk know its time had come?
It was ready to expire.

Why couldn't the skeleton laugh?
He was missing his funny bone.

What do you call someone with a hat made out of bones?
Bonehead.

Why did the zombie stop its car?
It reached a dead end.

Do zombies ever rest?
Of corpse they don't.

What do a bunch of ghosts playing baseball have?

Team spirit.

What is a skeleton's favorite part of Thanksgiving?

The wishbone.

What do ghosts read in their spare time?

Booooooooks.

How long was the rabbit gone?

The hole day.

Why were the skeletons shocked when they looked in the grave?

No body was there.

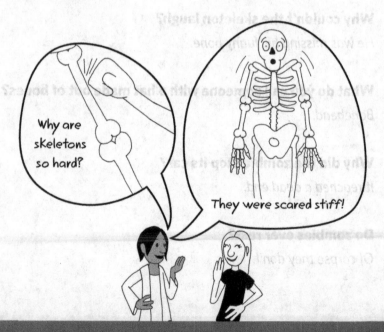

Why are skeletons so hard?

They were scared stiff!

How did all the colors become extinct?

They all dyed out.

What do you get when you cross a skeleton with a genie?

A wish bone.

What was the alphabet's favorite food?

Soup!

Why can't anyone sleep at a funeral?

Because it's a wake.

Was there any sign the candle was alive?

Just a flicker.

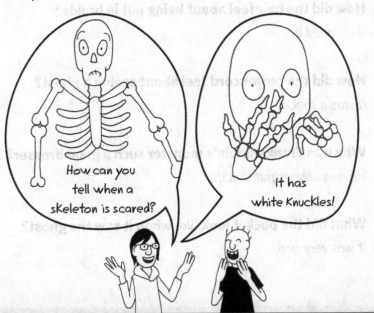

How can you tell when a skeleton is scared?

It has white Knuckles!

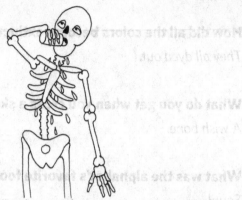

How can you tell when a skeleton needs a drink?

It's bone-dry!

Why was the broom confused?
It didn't know which witch was which.

How did the hair feel about being put in braids?
It dreaded it.

How did the power cord feel about seeing a ghost?
It was a shock.

Why was Frankenstein's monster such a good dresser?
He was always put together.

What did the bucket look like when it saw the ghost?
It was very pail.

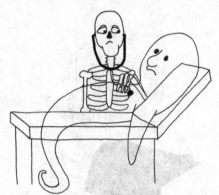

Why was the skeleton worried about the ghost?

He wasn't all there!

What is a ghost's favorite fruit?
Boo-berries!

How do you feel when you have lice?
Lousy.

What is a skeleton's favorite food?
Spare ribs.

What did the bunny think of the scary movie?
It was hare-raising.

Why wouldn't the wood go into the haunted house?
It was petrified.

What is a zombie's favorite time of the day?

Mourning!

Do cemetery workers like their job?

They dig it.

What did the train signal do to the zombie?

It stopped him dead in his tracks!

What did the snake do when it saw the ghost?

It jumped right out of its skin.

What happened when the vampire dropped his dinner?

He made a bloody mess.

How did the building know the ground was scared?

It was quaking.

Why were the two bears so different?

They were polar.

What were the turkeys so scared of?

The goblin'.

What did the windows do when they realized the house was haunted?

They shuttered!

Who works the graveyard shift?

The skeleton crew!

Who did the crying ghoul want?
Its mummie.

How come nobody wanted to hang out with the vampire?
He was a pain in the neck.

Which subject are witches best at?
Spelling.

How come witches' hats make them so clever?
They get the point.

Who was the nose the most afraid of?
The boogie man.

Why do ghosts make the best cheerleaders?

They have the most spirit!

How come vampires are never late for dinner?

Because they're punctural.

Why was the skeleton dead tired?

He worked the graveyard shift!

How come nobody likes to have dinner with a vampire?

It's too draining.

What did the wolf ask the moon?

Howl we ever get there.

What did the zombie do when it walked into a ceiling fan?

It lost its head.

Why did everyone laugh at the werewolf?

He was a howl.

What did the water do that was so scary?

It roared.

Why were the Zombies in a hurry to go to the party?

They were dying to meet everyone!

What do you call a vampire rock concert?

A monster jam!

How did the ghost feel about the love of her life?

She was errie-sistible.

How did the witch put a curse on the hive?

With a spelling bee.

Why was the Wicked Witch sent to her room?

She had a meltdown.

What do you do with a hot ghost?

Phantom.

What did Frankenstein's monster think of his bolts?

They were a pain in the neck.

What did the skeleton tell
the sheets about their secret?

Mummies the word!

What do you call a really scared cow?

A Coward.

Why did the ghosts have to leave the ball game?

They were booing everyone.

What kind of shampoo does Medusa use?

Snake Heads and Shoulders.

What do you get when you cross a vampire with a beagle?

A bloodhound.

Why was the Minotaur so stubborn?

Because he was bullheaded.

Why are zombies such good workers?

They are very deadicated!

Who is the biggest horse fly?

Pegasus.

How does Bigfoot tell time?

With a Sasqwatch.

What did one unicorn say to the other?

I get the point.

Why was Frankenstein's monster so unhappy?

He had two left feet.

How do ghosts handle their problems?

They try to see through them.

How were things looking for the headstone?

Very grave!

How did Frankenstein's monster feel about his surgery?

He was scarred for life.

How can you tell when a leprechaun is jealous?

He's green with envy.

How come no one likes to listen to Puff's stories?

Because he would always drag on.

Why didn't anyone invite the dementors to the party?

Because they sucked the life out of the room.

How come no one took the centaur seriously?

Because he was always horsing around.

2
ANIMAL INSTINCTS—Stinky Animals, Bathroom Jokes, etc.

What do you call a monkey that farts in church?

A badboon.

Why did the rooster call in sick?

He had the cock-a-doodle-flu.

Did you hear about the lion with diarrhea?
It was a cat-astrophe.

How can you tell the difference between elephant and rhinoceros poop?
Elephants work for peanuts.

Why don't monkeys get constipated?
Because they are always in the swing of things.

Why do lap dogs have the worst-smelling poop?
Because they are so spoiled.

What does a dog call a litter box?

All-you-can-eat buffet.

What do dogs call fire hydrants?

Public toilets.

Did you hear the joke about squirrel poop?

It was really nutty.

What is the most difficult animal to hold a conversation with?

A goat because they always butt in.

Why did the chicken cross the road?
To get to the bathroom.

What's invisible and smells like bananas?
Monkey farts.

What dog has the most germs?
Bac-terrier.

What do a race track and your little brother's underwear have in common?

They're both covered in skid marks.

Why did the armadillo cross the road?
To show that he had guts.

Why do worms make good detectives?

They know how to get to the bottom of things.

Where does a baseball player rub toilet paper?

On his bat.

What do you get when a cat has a cold?
Mew-cus.

A bear and a rabbit are pooping in the woods. The bear asked the rabbit, "Do you have problems with poop sticking to your fur? The rabbit, a little confused, replied, "No." "That's great!" said the bear as he grabbed the rabbit and started wiping.

Why do animals eat their meat raw?
Because they are terrible cooks.

Why did the pig pee all over his pen?
He wanted to go hog wild.

What's another name for cow poop?

Beef patties.

What does pig poop smell like?

It stoinks!

What do dogs call vomit?

Second dinner.

What do you get from a nauseated cow?

Spoiled milk.

What smells like ham and filth?
Pig farts.

What's red, chunky, and smells like a gazelle?
Cheetah puke.

Which monster will make the biggest mess out of your bathroom?
The Loch Mess Monster.

What does a skunk say when you turn it inside out?
"Ouch!"

What gets better with age?
Dog poop.

What does bear poop smell like?
Unbearable.

What did the circus monkey say when the clown farted?

Nothing . . . it smelled so funny he couldn't stop laughing long enough to say anything!

What do you call a dinosaur that farts too much?

Stinky-saurus.

How do chickens know it's time to poop?

They use a cluck.

What cat loves beans the most?

Puss n´ toots.

What do dogs call it when they poop in their crate?

Midnight snack.

What are grizzly bear farts like?

Silent but violent.

Why do horses fart when they gallop?

They wouldn't achieve full horsepower if they didn't.

How do you keep a skunk from smelling?

Hold its nose.

Why didn't the pig laugh at the loud fart?

Because he was being a real boar.

What is orange and smells like peanuts?

Elephant puke.

How did the skunk feel after being run over by a car?

Smelly and tired.

What's brown, jumps, and lives in Australia?

Kangapoo.

What is a fly's favorite dessert?

Cow pie.

Two girls were walking in the woods. They came across a pile of dog poop. "Is that dog poop?" the first girl asked. "Smells like dog poop," said the other. Then they both put their finger in it. "Feels like dog poop." Then they both said, "Tastes like dog poop. Good thing we didn't step in it!"

Why did the vampire eat the dog?

He loves pupperonis.

Why was the pig covered in pimples?

OINKMENT
Pimple Remover
NEW!

It forgot to use medicated oinkment.

What do cows read when they're in the bathroom?
Cattle-logs.

What's invisible and smells like carrots and cabbage?
Rabbit farts.

Why did the cheetah eat the gazelle?
Because he loves fast food.

What do dogs call rabbit poop?
Easter eggs.

What do you call an elephant in a toilet bowl?

Stuck.

Did you hear about the girl who found electric eels in her toilet?

It was a shocking discovery!

How did the T-Rex feel after vomiting all night?

Dino-sore.

How do you make a pig fly?

Feed it a bowl of beans.

What do you call it when a dinosaur urinates?

Pee-rex.

What do cows pee?

Cheese Whiz.

Have you heard the one about the constipated lion?

Get ready to roar!

What's the most gassy fish in the ocean?
Puffer fish.

What did the skunk say to the farting man?

"No need to make such a stink, I've got you covered."

What should you do if pigs start to fly?

Get an umbrella.

Two bats hanging in their cave. The first bat asked the second, "Do you remember the worst day of your life?" The second bat replied, "Yeah. The day I had diarrhea!"

What do dogs call firemen?

Toilet repairmen.

What do you call poop you can't push out?

A frightened turtle.

Why was the crocodile's pee so yellow?

He drank too much gator-ade.

A bird in the hand . . . will probably poop in your hand.

What did the cat say when the dog that was trying to pee?

Looks like you need a leg up!

What animal is best at wiping itself clean?

An octopus.

Did you hear about the turkey with a flatulence problem?

It shot stuffing all the way across the Thanksgiving table.

How is a scientist like a fly?

They are both attracted to stools.

Why did the bear throw up after eating George Washington?

Because it is hard to keep a good man down.

Where do pigs "do their business"?
In a pork-a-potty.

What's green, slimy, and smells like peanuts?
Elephant puke.

Why did the pig farmer go to the hospital?
He caught a bad case of pink eye.

Why do fish record how much they pooped?
They always have scales.

Why did the turkey need a bath?
It smelled fowl.

Did you hear about the T-rex that didn't have the ability to fart?
It faced ex-stink-tion.

What animal always throws up after it eats?

A yak.

Did you hear about the sheep that went to the bathroom together?

They were tightly knit.

What is a vampire's favorite dog breed?

Bloodhound.

Why did the sick chicken cross the road?

To get to the odor side.

Did you hear about the cow with diarrhea?

It was an udder disaster!

Why did the Loch Ness monster eat the ship?

He was craving Captain Crunch.

3
CULTURE VULTURES—
Knock Knocks About Celebrities and Characters

Knock knock! *Who's there?*
Elmo. *Elmo who?*
You don't know who Elmo is?

Knock knock! *Who's there?*
Merilee. *Merilee who?*
Merilee we roll along, roll along, roll along . . .

Knock knock! *Who's there?*
Joanna. *Joanna who?*
Joanna build a snowman?

Knock knock! *Who's there?*
Bashful. *Bashful who?*
I can't say—I'm too embarrassed!

Knock knock! *Who's there?*
Thor. *Thor who?*
Thor-ry, wrong house!

Knock knock! *Who's there?*
Dora. *Dora who?*
Dora my way, or I'd come on in with Map and Swiper.

Knock knock! *Who's there?*
Art. *Art who?*
Art-who-D-2. Beep-boop!

Knock knock! *Who's there?*
Dallas. *Dallas who?*
Dallas in Wonderland!

Knock knock! *Who's there?*
Alito. *Alito who?*
Alito of the pack.

Knock knock! *Who's there?*
Diarrhea. *Diarrhea who?*
Diarrhea wimpy kid.

Knock knock! *Who's there?*
Grinch. *Grinch who?*
Grinch who stole Christmas!

Knock knock! *Who's there?*
Siri. *Siri who?*
Siri, wrong house!

Knock knock! *Who's there?*
Yah. *Yah who?*
No, I use Google.

Knock knock! *Who's there?*
Fantastic Four. *Fantastic Four who?*
Fantastic Four you to let us in already!

Knock knock! *Who's there?*
Jacqueline. *Jacqueline who?*
Jacqueline Hyde.

Knock knock! *Who's there?*
Eeyore. *Eeyore who?*
Eeyore not letting me in, and that makes me sad!

Knock knock! *Who's there?*
Milhouse. *Milhouse who?*
Milhouse is empty, can I come hang out with you for a while?

Knock knock! *Who's there?*
Popeye. *Popeye who?*
Popeye wanna talk to you, you in there with Ma?

Knock knock! *Who's there?*
Tintin. *Tintin who?*
Tintin happen to leave the door unlocked, I guess.

Knock knock! *Who's there?*
Shrek. *Shrek who?*
You Shrek me to stand out here all day and wait for you?

Knock knock! *Who's there?*
Mickey Mouse. *Mickey Mouse who?*
Mickey Mouse not be the right one, because I can't seem to unlock the door!

Knock knock! *Who's there?*
Romeo. *Romeo who?*
Romeo-nly me and Juliet out here!

Knock knock! *Who's there?*
Sherlock Holmes. *Sherlock Holmes who?*
Sherlock Holmes up, or somebody could break in.

Knock knock! *Who's there?*
Tigger. *Tigger who?*
Tigger treat!

Knock knock! *Who's there?*
Snow. *Snow who?*
There's snow place like home!

Knock knock! *Who's there?*
Only. *Only who?*
Only you can prevent forest fires!

Knock knock! *Who's there?*
Oz. *Oz who?*
Oz just about to tell you if you'd give me a second.

Knock knock! *Who's there?*
Narnia. *Narnia who?*
Narnia business.

Knock knock! *Who's there?*
Pink Panther. *Pink Panther who?*
Pink Panther all I have to wear, I better do some laundry!

Knock knock! *Who's there?*
Juicy. *Juicy who?*
Juicy that new movie trailer?

Knock knock! *Who's there?*
Sombrero. *Sombrero who?*
Sombrero-ver the rainbow . . .

Knock knock! *Who's there?*
Rupert. *Rupert who?*
Rupert your left foot in, Rupert your left foot out . . .

Knock knock! *Who's there?*
Ivan. *Ivan who?*
Ivan working on the railroad . . .

Knock knock! *Who's there?*
Captain Jack. *Captain Jack who?*
Captain Jack-ed your stuff. He is a pirate, after all.

Knock knock! *Who's there?*
Kermit. *Kermit who?*
Grab Kermit and a ball, and let's play catch!

Knock knock! *Who's there?*
Deduct. *Deduct who?*
Donald Deduct, quack-quack!

Knock knock! *Who's there?*
Sloane. *Sloane who?*
Sloane Ranger. Hi-ho, Silver!

Knock knock! *Who's there?*
Yachts. *Yachts who?*
Eh, yachts up, Doc?

Knock knock! *Who's there?*
Pooh. *Pooh who?*
Don't cry, I'm a friendly bear.

Knock knock! *Who's there?*
Moana. *Moana who?*
Moana come in for a while?

Knock knock! *Who's there?*
Belle. *Belle who?*
No, there's no need for ballyhoo, it's just me.

Knock knock! *Who's there?*
Mater. *Mater who?*
See you Mater, alligator!

Knock knock! *Who's there?*
Chicken Little. *Chicken Little who?*
The sky is falling!

Knock knock! *Who's there?*
Nemo. *Nemo who?*
Nemo knock-knock jokes? I've got plenty!

Knock knock! *Who's there?*
Mr. Incredible. *Mr. Incredible who?*
Mr., it's incredible you haven't let me in yet!

Knock knock! *Who's there?*
Jughead. *Jughead who?*
Jughead-ed out real soon!

Knock knock! *Who's there?*
Josie. *Josie who?*
Just Josie, no Pussycats.

Knock knock!
Who's there?
Bond. *Bond who?*
Bond to succeed if you keep trying!

Knock knock! *Who's there?*
Smurfette. *Smurfette who?*
Smurfette all the smurfberries!

Knock knock! *Who's there?*
Fozzie. *Fozzie who?*
Fozzie last time, these are supposed to be funny! Wocka-wocka-wocka!

Knock knock! *Who's there?*
Gumby. *Gumby who?*
Gumby banned at school, so you better not bring any!

Knock knock! *Who's there?*
Hello Kitty. *Hello Kitty who?*
Hello Kitty, do you want some tuna?

Knock knock! *Who's there?*
Dory. *Dory who?*
Hi, I'm Dory. Want to hear a knock-knock joke?

Knock knock!
Who's there?
Richie Rich.
Richie Rich who?
Richie Rich you could at least say hi.

Knock knock!
Who's there?
Road Runner.
Road Runner who?
Beep-beep!

Knock knock!

Who's there?

Chip 'n' Dale.

Chip 'n' Dale who?

Chip, 'n', Dale cover the rest.

Knock knock!

Who's there?

Batman.

Batman who?

Just Batman. I work alone.

Knock knock! *Who's there?*
Remy. *Remy who?*
Remy come in there and make you some dinner!

Knock knock! *Who's there?*
Stitch. *Stitch who?*
Stitch you hear I like you?

4
RIDDLED WITH FUN—Famous Characters, etc.

How do cars eat?

Off their license plates!

Why did Mr. Potato Head look so sad?

Because his mouth was on upside down.

Why did the circus performer get so tired at work?

He was juggling two jobs.

What kind of haircuts do sponges get?

Bobs.

Why did the snake get lost?

It was rattled!

What do you get when you combine a pirate and a bird?
A Jack Sparrow.

What do you get when you cross Bozo with a goldfish?
A clown fish.

How does Count Dracula play baseball?
With a vampire bat.

Why was Mr. Potato Head so embarrassed?
He picked someone else's nose.

What is Shaggy's favorite hobby?
Scooby diving.

What do you call Princess Sofia's problems?

A royal mess!

If a mountain and a valley had a baby, what would they name it?
Cliff.

What is Anna and Elsa's favorite game?
Freeze tag.

What happens when Sponge Bob pretends to be a pirate?
He walks the plankton.

Which bunny can drive you crazy?
Bugs.

What did Puss do when someone complimented his shoes?
He gave them the boot.

Why was the tree so loud?

It had a lot of bark!

How did Donatello the Ninja Turtle finally get a girlfriend?
He finally came out of his shell.

How did the Seven Dwarfs feel about being short?
They under-stood completely.

What was the first thing Thomas did with his dog when he brought it home?
He trained it.

Why did the king believe the knight's story?
He sword it was true.

What did the skunk say to the only pink cat it had ever seen?
Hello, kitty.

How can you tell if a cartoon is happy?

It's very animated.

Where do chicken jokes come from?

The funny farm.

What one word can change everything?

Abracadabra.

What do you call a clown who wears his nose on his ear?

A Bozo.

Why are pickles so slow?

They tend to dill-y-dally.

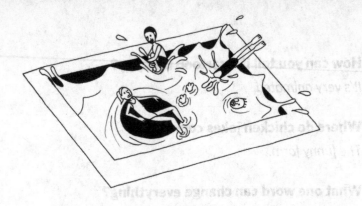

How did the kids like the swimming pool?

It made a big splash!

Where do pigs go to get clean?
The hogwash.

Why was the bowling ball wet?

There was rain in the gutters

How do bees communicate?

They use buzz words!

Where did Loopsy go on her trip?

To La La Land.

How do canyons eat?

They gorge themselves.

Why was the door so nervous?

It was unhinged.

How did the pig get out of the mud?

It was snort of a problem.

When is your hair noisy?

When it has bangs.

Why did the water have to calm down?

It spouted off.

How many friends did the bell bring to the party?

It brought the whole clang.

What do baby brooks do?

Babble.

Why was the toilet red?

It was flushed.

How does a runner drink milk?

She laps it up.

What does Barbie think about while she is sleeping?

Her dream home!

How does a tongue draw attention to itself?

When it sticks out!

What do trains hang on to when they go downstairs?
The rails.

How do you know when a bell has something to say?
It chimes in.

Why did the percussionists have to take a break?
They were drumming up some trouble.

What happened to the mad scientist's plan?
It fizzled out.

What do tunes say when they're stumped?
Hum.

Which cartoon character spends
the most time on Twitter?

Tweety Bird!

Why was the nail in bed?
It had a pounding headache.

What did the pot do with the chili's secret?
It spilled the beans.

How did the chicken do at impersonating a duck?
Just clucky.

How did the road feel about twin chickens crossing it?
Sort of double-crossed.

Why wouldn't the cube go to the show?
It was a blockbuster.

What did the doorknob say to the door?
It's my turn.

Why did the potato chip stop the car?
There was a dip in the road.

What do plastic bags wear on formal occasions?
Zip ties.

What room did the racket stay in?
10 S.

What sport was the bank good at?
Vaulting.

What did the butter say to Mr. Potato Head?

You make me melt!

What would the tree do if it had a window?

Add a little shade!

What do you call a silly pickle?
A daffy dill.

Why couldn't the boxing gloves get along?
They weren't a good match.

Why did the pickles climb into the truck?
The door was ajar.

Why are pianos good with locks?
They have a lot of keys.

Where do toilet paper rolls sleep?
Under the sheets.

What did Anna do when she forgot
her part in the show?

She froze!

What did the juicer do to the lemons?

Gave them some ade.

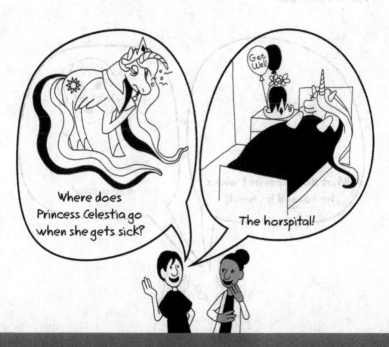

Where does
Princess Celestia go
when she gets sick?

Get Well

The horspital!

Why do flowers work out?

They don't want to be pansies.

Why was the fir tree so sad?

He pined for the other tree the moment he cedar.

What did the pumpkins think of the other crop?

It was a little corny.

Why was the necklace so bored?

It was tired of hanging around.

What's the best way to listen to fireworks?

With a boom box.

What did Casper get when he banged his head?

A boo-boo!

What happened when the laundry started wrestling?

The clothes were pinned.

What does a hero eat his soup out of?

A super bowl.

What did the lamp post on its page?

Something enlightening.

Where do snowmen go to dance?

Snow balls.

Why did the shrub quit working?

It was bushed.

What were the two garden hoses expecting?

A little squirt!

Why did the candle get sent to its room?

It had a meltdown!

Why was the coffee so upset?
Someone mugged it.

Why was the tennis ball shocked?
Someone took it to court.

What happened when the quilt told the needle a joke?
He had her in stitches.

Did the drill finally finish its supper?
Every last bit.

Why did the officer stop the yarn?
It was weaving in and out of traffic.

What did the Transformer tell
the waitress as it was leaving?

Keep the change!

How do you know when your dishes are in trouble?

They're in hot water.

What was Rumpelstiltskin doing in the Olympics?

Going for the gold.

How come the Tin Man never needed a bath?

He was always squeaky clean.

What do you call a tiny onion?

A Minion.

How did Sponge Bob like being in the pool?

He soaked it up.

How did Oh save the Boovs?

He had a good Tip.

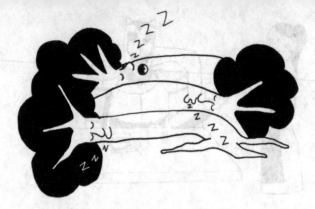

How do trees sleep?
Like logs!

What do you get when you cross a beetle and a rabbit?
Bugs Bunny.

How come Jacques made Nemo go through "The Ring of Fire"?
Because he was shellfish.

What did the ogre do about all of his problems?
Shrekked them off.

What do you get when you cross a black sheep with a baby cat?
A Baaad Kitty.

How did Mator's friend get around?
Like lightning.

5
WHERE ARE WE?—Cities, Countries, Locations, etc.

Where do trees come from?
Oaklahoma.

Why'd they name it Wyoming?

Because wy not?

Did you know that Wisconsin has an unmarried daughter?

You can call her Miss Consin.

What's the heaviest state?
Mass-achusetts.

What state makes the most writing utensils?

Pencil-vania.

Did you know they made a sequel to Oregon?

It's called Moregon.

Did you hear the chocolate lover moved to Alaska?

He heard that it was full of mousse.

Lots of people want to visit the
Netherlands and buy clogs.
Wooden shoe?

What state is always the most prepared and best dressed for sports?

New Jersey.

Why is there only one Arizona?

Arizona room for the one.

If there were only three more states, we'd have 53.

And then we'd truly be one nation indivisible!

Why is England so wet?
The queen has had a long reign.

Did you hear that the Italian airline messed up and forgot to charge a plane full of passengers?

They were free to Rome!

What's the fastest-growing city in the world?

Dublin.

Did you know that England doesn't have any blood banks?

Sure, but at least it has a Liverpool.

Her: Do you really think I'm from South America?

Him: Yes, I Bolivia.

What's the most fast-paced city in the world?

Moscow. Everyone there is Russian.

What's the wealthiest city in Virginia?

Richmond.

Why is it called Washington, D.C.?

Because D C is just to the east.

There are so many lightning storms in Australia.

That's why they call it the land down thunder.

What's the oiliest place on Earth?

Greece.

What's the tallest building in your city?

The library, because it's got a lot of stories.

In which California city can you buy a really fancy Dodge Caravan?

Van Nuys.

Why are French goats so musically talented?
Because they're born with French horns.

Unless you visit Helsinki on your Scandinavian vacation, your trip remains un-Finnished.

When they told me La Paz was a capital city, I said, "I don't Bolivia."

Usually the only time CNN reports on anything in Norway it's Oslo news day.

Why are mountains the funniest place to visit?
Because they're hill areas!

Is there Nintendo in France?
Wii!

I went to a fancy English hotel.
Or, rather, a great Brit inn.

Where do the queen's dogs live?
In Barkingham Palace.

What state is great for dipping?
Oklahummus.

What state comes in a can packed with water?
Tunasee.

In what state would you find the most pigs?
New Hamshire.

Which state has excellent-smelling breath?
Vermint.

Which state is easiest to drive in?
Road Island.

When traveling to Central America, remember your manners.

Always say Belize and thank you.

I liked visiting Oceania, and I'd love to travel there Samoa.

What's the best way to talk to Vikings?
You better learn Norse Code.

She said she was from a country in the Middle East.

No, really, she's Syria's!

What's part of the United Kingdom and full of water?

Wales.

It would be fun to go the Emerald Isle.

Irish I could go this summer!

I can't wait to visit Africa.

I'm Ghana go later this year.

What state is the best to celebrate Thanksgiving in?
Kenturkey.

Want to go visit the most northern state?
Juneau you want to.
When I buy tickets, Alaska!

There's a giant country right above the United States.
Canada believe it?

I went to southeast Asia and it was so beautiful I felt weak Indonesia.

CapeTown Driver's License

S97347123
DOB
7/8/1996

Super Guy
100 Hero Street
Cape Town

Where do superheroes come from?
Cape Town.

What Dutch city is full of cute and fuzzy rodents?

Hamsterdam.

What makes up the city of Boston?

About two thousand bospounds.

Never play Hide and Seek with a mountain.

They always peak!

My grandparents went on vacation to Cuba.
I hear they're Havana good time.

What's a better name for a food court when you're on a diet?

A craveyard.

What kind of music might you hear in space?

Neptunes.

What's another name for a dentist's office?

A filling station.

Those two volcanoes over there are inseparable.
It's true lava!

What do you call a hug in Paris?

A French press.

Where do police officers like to eat?

At the arrestaurant.

A cruise ship is really just another name for a boatel.

Why are barns so noisy?

The goats have horns.

Where do astronauts get their astronaut training?
Mooniversity.

What stands overlooking New York and sneezes all day?
The A-Choo! of Liberty.

What European monument can't stand up?
The I-Fell Tower.

Where do termites go on vacation?
Hollywood!

Where do wasps go on vacation?
Stingapore.

Where do locks go on vacation?
Key West.

What's the world's laziest mountain?

Ever-rest.

What kind of hotels will birds stay in?

Anything cheep.

Where do shoelaces go on vacation?

Tie-land.

Where do ghosts go to relax?
The Boo-Hamas.

Where do shoes go on vacation?

Lace Vegas.

Where do pirates go on vacation?

Arrrrrrgentina.

What's the coldest place in South America?

Chile.

What do you call a bird stuck at the North Pole?
A brrrrrrrd.

Where do viruses go on vacation?

Germ-any.

In what state will you find the most lions?

Mane!

What's the most popular game show in the ocean?

Whale of Fortune.

What's the easiest kind of building to lift?
A lighthouse.

What state is full of cats and dogs and hamsters and gerbils?

Petsylvania.

Did you hear about the kid who ran all the way from New York to California?

He needed to West.

Why was the horse from Kentucky so generous to his horse friends?

Southern horspitality.

Where do zombies go for a swim?
The Dead Sea.

Did you hear about the cheese factory that exploded in France?

There was nothing but des brie.

Did you hear about the crime in the parking garage?

It was wrong on so many levels.

What planet is like a circus?

Saturn—it has three rings!

What's the most popular pop in the Midwest?

Mini-soda.

Where do ghosts go for a swim?
Lake Erie.

They may look far apart on a map, but Ireland is just one C away from Iceland.

If you want to live in Australia and eat eucalyptus leaves all day, you have to have the right koalifications.

Why is Tel Aviv a great vacation spot?

Because it Israeli fun there!

Her: I just climbed to the top of the world's biggest mountain.

Him: Wow, Everest?

Her: Sure, about every 100 feet or so.

Eating while traveling through Europe is very important.

Otherwise, when people get Hungary they're nothing Budapest.

There was a big historical event that rocked the Southern United States.

Many states witnessed it, and since they're so close to each other . . .

whatever Tennessee, Arkansas.

The Pacific Ocean met up with the Atlantic Ocean in Panama.

They didn't say anything—but they waved.

The Flintstones varies in popularity in the Middle East.

Not many people in Dubai like it, but the folks in Abu Dhabi do.

The best views in Paris are atop that famous tower.

You can certainly get an Eiffel!

I knew a guy who took a job in Seoul.

He thought it would be a good Korea move.

How come the astronaut never returned to the moon?
He wanted to give it some space.

A small area of undeveloped land may not seem like much.

But to me, it's a lot.

Kid: How come the moon was full the other day, but now it's just a crescent?
Mom: I wouldn't worry about it—it's just a phase.

I didn't used to want to visit that famous tower in Pisa.

But I think now I'm leaning toward it.

I went to a great concert in Hawaii.

The people were dancing in the isles!

6
QUICK PICKS—
Boogers, Snot, etc.

The Snail: A long slimy trail of snot.

What do boogers and nerds have in common?

People like to pick on them.

What's a nose's favorite movie?

Boogie Nights

What do you call a wall of boogers?

A picket fence.

Why was the nose so sad?

Because it was always getting picked on.

What's full of boogers and smells?

A nose.

Did you hear about the booger who liked to gossip?

He was pretty nosy.

What's the difference between boogers and Brussels sprouts?

No one eats Brussels sprouts.

Why did the little boy only eat boogers?

He was a picky eater.

What do you call a booger that's been on a diet?

Slim Pickins.

Did you hear the nose got back together with a bunch of snot?

It was an old phlegm.

What did the ear overhear the other ear saying?
There's something between us that smells.

TYPES OF SNOT

• **Chunky Monkey:** *When you have hard boogers stuck on top of slimy boogers.*

• **The Phantom:** *When you pick one and it just . . . disappears.*

• **The Nose Dandruff:** *A dry, flaky booger that just kind of falls out of your nose of its own volition.*

• **The Fugitive:** *A booger that you just can't seem to grab, and it gets farther and farther up there and out of reach.*

• **Dracula's Delight:** *Bloody boogers.*

• **The Clinger:** *A booger that just won't come loose, no matter how hard you try.*

• **Tenacious B:** *A booger that you try to flick away, but it won't budge, or even worse, it moves over to the other finger you're using to flick it off.*

• **The Old-Timer:** *A booger that's so old and dry that it's gone from green to gray.*

• **The Trophy:** *A booger so big that took you so long to get out that you kind of want to show it off to everybody.*

• **The Mysterious Cave:** *When you pick your nose because it's irritated and there aren't any boogers or snot in there at all.*

What does a booger say to his girlfriend?
I'm stuck on you.

The Broken Faucet: When you 've got a cold or allergies and you lean over and a bunch of snot just pours right out of your nose.

Where do boogers go on vacation?

Snotland!

Why do we have fingernails?

So we can dig deeper!

What do you say to your friend when they're hungry?

Go to Booger King.

What do you get if you put peppers in your nose?

A hot boogie.

Why did the booger and the pimple team up?

They were sick of being picked on!

Why is there no such thing as an empty nose?

Because even a clean one has fingerprints.

Did you hear about the guy who could pick his nose, dance, and play the trumpet all at the same time?

They called him the Boogie Woogie Bugle Boy.

What button stinks most?

A belly button.

Why did the loogey die of old age?

Because slime flies!

Did you hear about the guy whose nose ran for three months straight?

Snot funny.

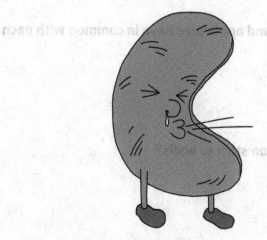

Which nut has the worst allergies?

Cashew.

Where can you find someone who's never picked their nose?
Nowhere. That person has never existed.

How are boogers and fruits similar?
Both get picked and eaten.

What did the booger say when the magician asked for a volunteer?
Pick me! Pick me!

What do noses and apple pies have in common with each other?
They're both crusty.

What monster can stick to walls?
The boogeyman.

What did the booger's dad say to his son when he talked back?

Don't be snotty with me!

What's thick, slimy, and hangs from tall trees?

Giraffe snot.

What was the nose so melancholy about?

It didn't get picked.

What's inside of a haunted spirit's nose?

Booogers.

What do you call a ball of snot wearing a motorcycle helmet?

A snail!

What's yellow, sticky, and smells like bananas?

Monkey snot.

What's a booger's favorite casino in Vegas?

The Golden Nugget.

What do you call the biggest booger in the world?

Green Giant.

He wanted a quarter-pounder for lunch.

Why did the elephant pick his nose?

Fancy Words for Boogers (for when you need to be dignified about your bodily functions)

Nostril Pickings

Gold Dust

Hidden Gems

Upper Crusts

Boogeaux

Nasal Soil

What do noses and brie cheese have in common?

They both smell and get runny.

What do you call a Roman emperor with a cold?

Julius Sneezer.

What did the kid say to the booger?
It's been nice gnawing you.

Why did John hate his nose?
Because it didn't smell very good.

What do toenails and cheese have in common?
Their smell.

Where did the gross girl save her fingernails?

In a nail file.

Who is the snottiest writer?

Ian Phleming.

What did the gross magician say when he picked at his pimple?

Scabracadabra!

What did the finger do when the nose went on strike?

Picket.

What do you call a knight with bad acne?

Sir Picks-a-lot.

What runs in most families?
Noses.

What is dandruff's favorite cereal?
Anything with flakes.

A little boy picked his nose, then licked his finger. His father noticed him doing it and said, "Son, stop that! That is absolutely disgusting!" Then he took a tissue and wiped the booger off is finger. "Hey, I should be the one mad at you," the boy said. "And why is that?" his father asked. "I didn't get to flick it, and that's the most fun part!"

What is another name for snowman dandruff?

Frosted Flakes.

What did the diabetic woman find in her nose?

A sugar booger.

What is a gross boy's favorite food?

Hamboogers.

Why was the nose so excited?

Because it was time to boo-gie woogie.

Receipt

Subtotal: $30.00
Tax: $ 3.00

Total $33.00

Tip:

Total: $33.00

What do you leave a for a waiter whose
ears are full of gunk?

A Q-tip.

Did you hear about the girl with too much earwax?

It was downright ear-ie.

What's the best part about flossing your teeth?

Finding all the free snacks for later!

What do zits drink?

Pop.

What should you never eat if a person with dandruff gives it to you?

A powdered doughnut.

What do you call a little zit?

A simple pimple.

What do Italian teenagers eat?

Zit-i.

Why should you not worry when you get a pimple?

Because zit happens.

Did you hear about the really tall guy with dandruff?

The mayor thought it was snowing and ordered the schools canceled.

Why didn't anyone want to hang out with Dandruff Dave?

He was really flaky.

I remember when my ears used to be a lot filthier.

Sorry, I was just waxing nostalgic.

Did you hear about the guy who had a massive waxy buildup in his head?

It was earful, just earful!

What's worse than having an ear full of earwax?

Having an ear full of earwigs.

What do you do if you see a hardworking booger?

Pick it!

EAR WAX MONIKERS

- *Sticky icky.*

- *Ear turds.*

- *Headphone honey.*

- *Witches' butter.*

Did you hear about the kid who had really smelly armpits?

His teacher gave him a D because he never raised his hand in class.

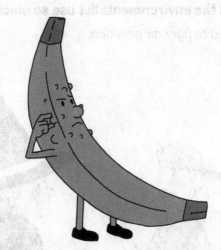

What's the difference between a banana and a pimple?

One bruises easily, the other oozes easily.

What did the pimple say to the butt?

"I'm tired of people picking on us!"

What's another name for a slug?

Look in your nose.

What do mean girls do to dandruff?

Give it the cold shoulder.

Why did the environmentalist use so much mouthwash?

He wanted to fight air pollution.

What did the bro say to the witch?

"Wart's up?"

How can you tell when your scissors get mad?

They're a little snippy!

What comes between before school and after school?
Middle school.

Why couldn't the crayon see anything?
It blacked out!

Why was the ruler so confused?
It couldn't think straight.

What did one ruler say when the other ruler was leaving?
So long!

What do you call it when there's nothing on your math homework?
No problem.

Why couldn't the second class of kids get on the plane?
They only had room for the first class.

Why were the scissors smiling?
Because they had their work cut out for them.

Why did the red marker get in trouble for writing in the book?
Because it red it all by itself.

What are the best steps to take to solve a really hard math problem?

The steps up to your teacher's desk.

Why was the dot-to-dot struggling?

It couldn't seem to connect.

What's another name for counterfeit money?

Play dough.

Why did the newspaper struggle in school?

It was having trouble with its Times tables.

What do you call a thermometer that doesn't pass its test?

A failed a-temp.

Why did the cowboy have to leave school?

For horsing around too much!

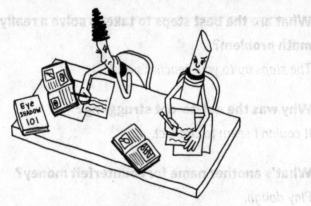

Why did the lipstick and mascara
have to stay after school?

To do makeup work!

What did the snowman learn about?

Numb brrrrs!

What do you call dirt that isn't real?

Play ground.

How did the cars do in school?

They didn't pass.

Why did the sheet music do well on a test?

It had taken notes.

How did the eagle do in school?

It soared.

How did the rainbow do in school?

It passed with flying colors.

How did the carpenters do in school?
They finished.

How did the boat do in school?
It sailed through.

How did the road do at coloring?
It stayed inside the lines.

What did the bookshelves do at school?
They learned their upper and lower cases.

How did the shovel do in school?
It ditched a few classes.

What did the baggie do when the teacher told him no more talking?

He zipped it up!

Why couldn't the ice cream give a speech?

Because it froze!

Which part of school is a farmer's favorite?

Field trips.

How did the computer programs do in school?

They excelled.

How was school for the traffic light?

A little stop and go.

How was school for the concrete?

Really hard.

Why couldn't Humpty Dumpty wait for winter?

Because he had a great fall.

How did Bob the Builder do in school?

He nailed it.

What's a lawyer's favorite part of school?

Recess.

How did the fireman do in school?

Smoking.

What did one pencil say to the other?

You have a good point!

How did the king do in school?

He liked his subjects.

How did the phone do in school?

It got called on a lot for the answers!

Why did the bicycle do poorly in school?

He was two tired.

Why did the tennis player help the lunch lady?

He loved to serve.

Why was the tongue so special?

It stuck out.

How did the egg do in class?

It was a Grade-A student.

How did the music do in school?

Noteworthy.

Why did the giant have to stay after school?

He was in big trouble!

Why did the cafeteria flunk school?

It was always out to lunch.

Why did the doctors do well in school?

They gave it their best shot.

How come the football player is bad in art class?

He always tackles his projects.

How did the dancer do in class?

She tapped lightly around the subjects.

What was the beaker's favorite part of school?

That it graduated.

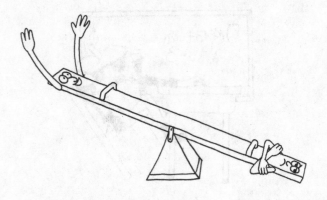

How did the seesaw feel from time to time?

It had its ups and downs!

How did the cat do in school?
Purrfect, because it was the teacher's pet.

Why did the hopscotch get in trouble?
It skipped class.

What was the movie's favorite part in school?
Extra credits.

How did the panda do in school?
It bearly made it.

How did the basketball do in school?
Slam dunk.

Why did the apple have to stay after school?

It was fresh!

How did Pacman like his classes?

He ate them up.

How did the apple do in school?

It was the teacher's favorite.

How come no one ate the cookies in the cafeteria?

Because they were crumby.

Why did the empty piggy bank flunk class?

Because he couldn't pay attention.

How did the candy do in school?

It fudged on its exam.

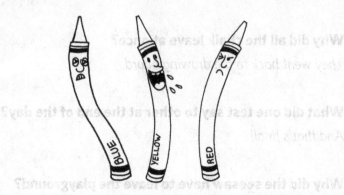

Which color is the loudest?

Yellow!

How did the history book do in school?

It past.

What kind of math do fish do in their schools?

Algaebra!

Why did all the chalk leave at once?

They went back to the drawing board.

What did one test say to other at the end of the day?

And that's final!

Why did the seesaw have to leave the playground?

It was a little unbalanced.

How do you know when a dog is bossy?

It barks orders.

Why did the chalk fall asleep in class?

It was really board.

How did the dog get through school?

It asked for yelp!

Why was the exam in a bad mood?

It was feeling a little testy!

What kind of paint do you use to paint a hand?
Finger paint!

Where do teachers live?
In school houses.

How long is a dollar's school year?
Four quarters.

Where do planks learn everything they need to know?
At boarding school.

When do owls learn the most?
At night school.

How did the baseball players do in school?

They knocked it out of the park!

What was the thermometer doing in school?
Getting its degree.

Why did they build onto the school cafeteria?
To give the lunch room.

What part of your eye goes to school?
Your pupil.

Why was the jump rope in timeout?
It skipped class.

Why are schools so full of energy?
They have a lot of pep rallies.

What did the doughnuts think about school?

They liked the hole thing!

How did the wand do at magic school?
He was a wizard at it.

How did the test disappear?
A student took it.

What do fish practice at their piano lessons?
Their scales.

Why was the finger in trouble?
For poking fun.

Why was the shoe late?
It was a little tied up.

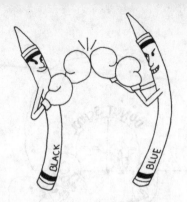

Which two colors hurt the most?

Black and blue!

Where do little plants go to learn?
Nursery schools.

Where do pens sleep?
Under sheets of paper.

Why didn't the rope show up to its exercise class?
It decided to skip it.

Why did the rotten milk always want more stuff?
It was spoiled.

Why did the brain get in trouble in school?
It was thinking out loud.

Why did the fish stay home from school?
It was feeling eel.

Knock knock! *Who's there?*
Yah. *Yah who?*
Yah who, let's party!

Knock knock! *Who's there?*
Sincerely. *Sincerely who?*
Sincerely this morning I've been waiting for you to open the door!

Knock knock! *Who's there?*
Miniature. *Miniature who?*
Miniature open your mouth, you'll say something silly!

Knock knock! *Who's there?*
Joe King. *Joe King who?*
Joe King you with another knock-knock!

Knock knock! *Who's there?*
District. *District who?*
District parents of yours means you probably can't come outside!

Knock knock! *Who's there?*
Chaos. *Chaos who?*
Chaos the letter that comes after J.

Knock knock! *Who's there?*
Riot. *Riot who?*
Riot on time!

Knock knock! *Who's there?*
Donohue. *Donohue who?*
Donohue think you can hide from me in there?

Knock knock! *Who's there?*
Duet. *Duet who?*
Duet right, or don't duet at all.

Knock knock! *Who's there?*
Hugh Cosmo. *Hugh Cosmo who?*
Hugh Cosmo trouble than anyone!

Knock knock! *Who's there?*
Oscar and Greta. *Oscar and Greta who?*
Oscar silly question . . . and Greta silly answer.

Knock knock! *Who's there?*
Carmen and Cohen. *Carmen and Cohen who?*
I can't tell if you're Carmen or Cohen.

Knock knock! *Who's there?*
Hello. *Hello who?*
My name's not who.

Knock knock! *Who's there?*
Toodle. *Toodle who?*
Toodle who to you too!

Knock knock! *Who's there?*
Gucci. *Gucci who?*
Gucci-gucci-goo!

Knock knock! *Who's there?*
Voodoo. *Voodoo who?*
Voodoo you think you are, anyway?

Knock knock! *Who's there?*
Polo. *Polo who?*
Polo-ver, you're under arrest!

Knock knock! *Who's there?*
Lotus. *Lotus who?*
Lotus in and we'll tell you.

Knock knock! *Who's there?*
Byte. *Byte who?*
Byte you're happy to see me again!

Knock knock! *Who's there?*
Amen. *Amen who?*
Amen hot water again.

Knock knock! *Who's there?*
Catch. *Catch who?*
Bless you!

Knock knock! *Who's there?*
Aldo. *Aldo who?*
Aldo anywhere with you!

Knock knock! *Who's there?*
Cain and Abel. *Cain and Abel who?*
Cain talk now . . . Abel tomorrow.

Knock knock! *Who's there?*
Datsun. *Datsun who?*
Datsun old joke.

Knock knock! *Who's there?*
Easter. *Easter who?*
Easter anybody home?

Knock knock! *Who's there?*
Myth. *Myth who?*
I myth seeing you.

Knock knock! *Who's there?*
Conrad. *Conrad who?*
Conrad-ulations, that was a great joke!

Knock knock! *Who's there?*
X. *X who?*
X me no questions, and I'll tell you no lies.

Knock knock! *Who's there?*
Yule. *Yule who?*
Yule be sorry!

Knock knock! *Who's there?*
Wendy Katz. *Wendy Katz who?*
Wendy Katz away, the mice will play!

Knock knock! *Who's there?*
Unaware. *Unaware who?*
Unaware is what you put on first!

Knock knock! *Who's there?*
Schick. *Schick who?*
Schick as a dog.

Knock knock! *Who's there?*
Sancho. *Sancho who?*
Sancho a letter, but you never replied.

Knock knock! *Who's there?*
Omega. *Omega who?*
Omega up your mind!

Knock knock! *Who's there?*
Megan, Elise, and Chicken. *Megan, Elise, and Chicken who?*
Megan, Elise, and Chicken it twice. Gonna find out who's naughty or nice . . .

Knock knock! *Who's there?*
Nana. *Nana who?*
Nana your business.

Knock knock! *Who's there?*
N.E. *N.E. who?*
N.E. body home?

Knock knock! *Who's there?*
Aloha. *Aloha who?*
Aloha myself in.

Knock knock! *Who's there?*
Flu. *Flu who?*
Hey, I wasn't crying!

Knock knock! *Who's there?*
Weird. *Weird who?*
Weird you go all day?

Knock knock! *Who's there?*
Scold. *Scold who?*
Scold out here!

Knock knock! *Who's there?*
Witch. *Witch who?*
Witch you would let me in!

Knock knock! *Who's there?*
Zombie. *Zombie who?*
The zombie who's going to break down your door!

Knock knock! *Who's there?*
Weirdo. *Weirdo who?*
Weirdo deer and the antelope play . . .

Knock knock! *Who's there?*
Waddle. *Waddle who?*
Waddle I do if you won't see me?

Knock knock! *Who's there?*
I won. *I won who?*
I won to suck your blooood!

Knock knock! *Who's there?*
Zombies. *Zombies who?*
Zombies make honey, others don't.

Knock knock! *Who's there?*
Believing. *Believing who?*
Open the door or I'll believing.

Knock knock! *Who's there?*
Disaster. *Disaster who?*
Disaster be my lucky day for once!

Knock knock! *Who's there?*
Insanity. *Insanity who?*
Don't you believe insanity Claus?

Knock knock! *Who's there?*
Says. *Says who?*
Says me, that's who!

Knock knock! *Who's there?*
Beezer. *Beezer who?*
Beezer black and yellow and live in a hive.

Knock knock! *Who's there?*
Decode. *Decode who?*
Decode is getting worse, open up!

Knock knock! *Who's there?*
Handsome. *Handsome who?*
Handsome of those cookies out here, I'm hungry!

Knock knock! *Who's there?*
Summertime. *Summertime who?*
Summertime you can be really funny, you know?

Knock knock! *Who's there?*
Oldest. *Oldest who?*
Oldest knocking is wearing me out!

Knock knock! *Who's there?*
Yellow. *Yellow who?*
Yellow! And how are you today?

Knock knock! *Who's there?*
Sizzle. *Sizzle who?*
Sizzle hurt you more than it hurts me!

Knock knock! *Who's there?*
Breed. *Breed who?*
Breed deep and say "aah!"

Knock knock! *Who's there?*
Wicked. *Wicked who?*
Wicked get dogs instead of cats, if you'd rather.

Knock knock! *Who's there?*
Value. *Value who?*
Value be my Valentine?

Knock knock! *Who's there?*
Noise. *Noise who?*
Noise to see you. How have you been?

Knock knock! *Who's there?*
Freeze. *Freeze who?*
**Freeze a jolly good fellow, freeze a jolly good fellow,
freeze a jolly good fellow . . . which nobody can deny!**

Knock knock! *Who's there?*
Argue. *Argue who?*
Argue going to let me in?!

Knock knock! *Who's there?*
Zany. *Zany who?*
Zany-body home?

Knock knock! *Who's there?*
Justice. *Justice who?*
Justice I thought!

Knock knock! *Who's there?*
Isolate. *Isolate who?*
Isolate to the party that I almost missed it!

Knock knock! *Who's there?*
Dispense. *Dispense who?*
Dispense are too tight, I think I gained weight!

Knock knock! *Who's there?*
Jig. *Jig who?*
Jig is up! You're under arrest!

Knock knock! *Who's there?*
Vilify. *Vilify who?*
Vilify knew my name, I'd tell you!

Knock knock! *Who's there?*
Calder. *Calder who?*
Calder cops, I've been robbed!

Knock knock! *Who's there?*
July. *July who?*
July awake at night?

Knock knock! *Who's there?*
Zagat. *Zagat who?*
Zagat says "meow."

Knock knock! *Who's there?*
Bertha. *Bertha who?*
Happy Bertha Day to you . . .

Knock knock! *Who's there?*
Ashley. *Ashley who?*
Ashley's foot is making my feet all gross!

Knock knock! *Who's there?*

Fangs. *Fangs who?*

Fangs for opening the door, I'm a vampire!

Knock knock! *Who's there?*

Senior. *Senior who?*

Senior through the keyhole, so I know you're in there.

Knock knock! *Who's there?*

Lucretia. *Lucretia who?*

Lucretia from the Black Lagoon!

Knock knock! *Who's there?*

Eyes darted. *Eyes darted who?*

Eyes darted to droop but I woke up!

Knock knock! *Who's there?*
Itch. *Itch who?*
Itch a long time coming!

Knock knock! *Who's there?*
Censor. *Censor who?*
Censor so smart, you tell me!

Knock knock! *Who's there?*
Vampire. *Vampire who?*
Vampire State Building!

Knock knock! *Who's there?*
Blue. *Blue who?*
Blue your nose on your sleeve again, huh?

What's a good name for a guy who works at a gas station? Phil!

Real Names of Hair Salons

Headmasters

Mane Attraction

Fort Locks

Shear Delight

Fresh Hair

Shear Madness

Blade Runners

Alive and Klippin'

Hair and Now

Hairoglyphics

Hair Necessities

Tortoise & The Hair

The Hairport

Cutting Remarks

The Mane Event

Cut 'N' Run

Curl Up and Dye

Hair On Earth

Headgames

Hair Today, Gone Tomorrow

Hair Raisers

Scissors Palace

Hairanoia

Politicians with Amusing Names

Janelle Lawless was a circuit court judge in Michigan.

Jay Walker ran for office in Pierce County, Georgia.

Dave Obey was a congressman from Wisconsin.

Timothy Shotwell ran for a sheriff position in Clark County, Washington.

Krystal Ball ran for office in Virginia in 2010. She didn't win . . . but she probably should have seen that coming.

What's a good name for a kid who lives in the bathroom? John!

Funny Beach House Names

Latitude Adjustment
Once Upon a Tide
Sea-Esta
What's Up Dock
Shore Thing
Family Tides
Beachy Keen
All Decked Out

What's a good name for a firefighter?
Ashley!

Sand Castle
Gimme a Break
Surf 'n' Sound
Dune Our Thing
Shore Fun
Seaclusion
Sunny Daze
Hide 'n' Sea
A Wave From It All
Wait 'n' Sea
Baywatch
Something Fishy

What's a good name for somebody who does yoga?
Matt!

When it comes to delivering her dialogue well, Anne Hathaway with words.

Which pop star makes rapid onstage wardrobe changes?
Tailor Swift.

Can you talk to your phone and ask it to do stuff?
No Siri.

What do you call a lady with a frog on her head?
Lily!

What's a good name for a person with a car on their head?

Jack!

What's a good name for a lady who wears a lot of red?

Scarlett!

What's a good name or someone who plays a stringed instrument?

Harper!

What's a good name for a girl who lives on the moon? Luna!

What's the difference between Christopher Columbus and the lid of a dish? One is a discoverer, the other is a dish coverer.

Syncing· · · ·

I changed my iPhone name to Titanic.
It's syncing now.

Truly there was no one in history who traveled and wandered around more than the Romans.

What do surfers wash their swim trunks in?
Tide.

A kid thought he was swimming in an ocean made out of orange soda.
It turns out it was just a Fanta sea.

What's a good name for someone who plays the flute? Piper!

Velcro is such a rip-off!

What's better in an emergency than an EMT?
A pair-a-medics.

Why did they call it the Dark Ages?
Because there were so many knights.

What's a good name for a tall girl?
Willow!

There was a robbery at the Apple Store, but they caught the guy because of an iWitness.

I, for one, like Roman numerals.

Why does the singer of "Chandelier" not want us to Sia?

Who is the sleepiest world leader in history?
Nap-oleon.

Einstein developed a theory about space.

And it was about time, too.

Every car that isn't an Acura is technically an Inacura.

Paul Revere always carried tissues.
He was, after all, the town crier.

What does Adele eat for dessert?

Jell-O.

How did Adele treat her sunburn?

Aloe.

What did Benjamin Franklin say when he discovered electricity? "I'm shocked!"

When the apple hit him on the head, Sir Isaac Newton understood the gravity of the situation.

Did you know that a chimp was once the president?
Ape-braham Lincoln!

How much does a hipster weigh?
An Insta-gram.

I was trying to take a picture when my friend
ran up and slathered Vaseline on my camera.
Now that's what I call a photo balm!

10
SPLATFEST

What do you say to someone who's
been throwing up all day long?

"Happy Barf-Day!"

Did you hear about the man who couldn't stop pooping and vomiting at the same time?

It's a pretty sick joke.

What do Italians call vomiting?

Barf-a-roni.

What happened to the teenager that drank eight sodas?

He threw 7UP.

What machine plays music so bad
it makes you want to vomit?

A pukebox.

What color is a belch?
Purple.

How does a burp cut loose and get a little crazy?
It goes out the other end.

What's soft and warm at bedtime but hard and stiff in the morning?
Vomit.

What did ancient Romans do in a vomitorium?
Un-wine.

Did you hear about the guy who missed the puke bucket and vomited all over the floor?
It was beyond the pail!

Did you hear about the professional golfer that was so nervous about the tournament that he threw up?
Suppose it's just barf for the course.

I just can't help telling jokes about vomiting.
What can I say, it's a sickness!

What do poets do in the bathroom?

They write poo-ems.

Do you want to hear a joke about vomit?
Coming right up!

Did you hear about the pilot who barfed on the plane?
He got through it with flying colors.

This is the last joke about vomiting.
I promise not to bring that up anymore.

Where is the most entertaining place to puke?

A hot air balloon...
Not so entertaining for anyone else though.

Why did the criminal enjoy vomiting?

Because it's ill-egal.

What is the most nauseating city?

Barf-celona.

How can you tell the difference between a healthy dog and a sick dog?

One barks, the other barfs.

Funny Puke Names

Liquidation sale

Spew

Tossing cookies

Lunch summons

Retching

Making stew

Feeding Poseidon

Porcelain offering

Pit stop at regurgitation station

Upchuck

Hurling

Liquid moan

Making monster food

Horking

Visiting the ejection seat

Blowing chunks

Yelling for Ralph

The ol' heave ho

Chunder

Chili storm

Blowing beans

Hugging the toilet

Hit the eject button

The urp burp

The technicolor yawn

What do dogs call their own vomit?

The soup course.

What did a burp say to the other?

Let's be stinkers and go backwards.

What's small, cuddly, and green?

A koala that needs to puke.

What beats throwing up out of a speeding car window?

Your heart.

Did you hear about the girl that puked up her lunch into the bowl?

No? I'll spare you.

What's worse than eating vomit soup?

Eating day-old vomit soup.

What airline does everyone get sick on?

Spew-nited.

What does a competitive eater do in the bathroom?

Prepares for battle.

Why wouldn't the billionaire take a shower?

Because she was filthy rich.

What happened when the kindergartener got sick during fingerprinting class?

She made a retch-a-sketch.

What did the chef say to the toilet?

One dinner, coming right up!

What do you get when you eat asparagus and cabbage?

The worst smelling bathroom of all time.

What flavor of ice cream will make you sick?

Van-ilta.

What special treat do you get the night of St. Patrick's Day?

A bowlful of lamb spew.

**HAVE A FRIEND CELEBRATING A BARFDAY?
HELP THEM GET INTO THE PARTY MOOD BY
SINGING THIS SONG!**

Happy barf day to you

You sat in my spew

Now you smell like vomit

Happy barf day to you

How did the bucket know he was about to vomit?

He was looking a little pail.

What's the best way to avoid getting sick in the car?

Roll down the window.

What's the difference between
puke and school lunch?

School lunch comes on a plate.

What does Thor wear on his bottom?
Thunderpants.

Why did the girl get sick at the haunted house?

It was too spew-key.

What stinks and flies through the air at 500 mph?

An airplane bathroom.

What do you call a bathroom in Finland?

Helstinki.

Clever ways to tell someone that they REALLY need to take a shower:

• *You smell worse than a city dump full of dog poop.*

• *You smell like you ate a big bowl of farts for lunch.*

• *You smell like you forgot to take off every diaper you wore when you were a baby.*

• *You smell like you forgot to throw away the toilet paper when you were done with it.*

• *You smell like you took a dump instead of leaving it behind.*

• *A gas station bathroom would think you smell bad.*

• *You smell like a cat confused you for a litter box.*

• *You make natural gas seem like anything but natural.*

• *You smell like a fart and poop had a race to see who could get out first, and they tied.*

• *Did you burp out of your butt and fart out of your mouth at the same time?*

Disgusting Titles Coming Soon to a Bookshelf Near You!

The Diarrhea Family *by Manny Luce-Bowles*

Dealing with Constipation *by U. R. Stuck*

How to Be a Proctologist *by Seymour Butz*

How to Properly Clean Yourself *by Duke E. Viper*

A History of Plumbers' Pants *by Sawyer Crack*

Vomiting Techniques *by Anya Neeze*

The Most Frequent Urination Problems *by P.P. de Ponce*

Common Rashes *by Mike Rauch-Burns*

Chronic Gas *by Ran Sidass*

11
THINGS AND STUFF—Silly Objects, Random Stuff, etc.

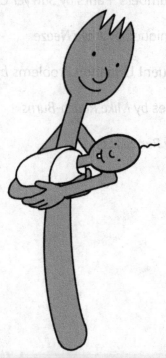

Where do baby spoons come from?
The spork.

Why did the computer crash?

It had a bad driver.

What's loud, musical, and keeps sweat out of your eyes?

A headband.

What has four wheels and flies?

A garbage truck.

Why was the calendar out late Friday night?

It had a date!

I've never seen a fossil so opposed to doing any work.
Talk about a lazy bones!

How come the mail arrived wet?

There was postage dew.

What's a better name for a fly swatter?

A splatula!

I just read this novel in Braille.

It was a feel-good story.

That metal wire got so upset over some minor thing.

It got all bent out of shape over nothing!

How do space cowboys see in the dark?
Saddle lights.

Have you ever met that really funny sewing machine?

It keeps everyone in stitches.

What did the pencil say to the knife?

"You sure are looking sharp today!"

What did the paper say to the pencil?

"You have a good point."

It's time to sell your vacuum cleaner.

It's just gathering dust.

Why did the woodsman put on pajamas?
He was invited to a lumber party.

While it cost a lot of money at Halloween, that mask has no face value.

"Wow, look at that ceiling! What a great paint job! It's so high up there!"
–Ceiling fans

He didn't use to like masking tape.
Then he became very attached to it.

Who steals soap out of bathtubs?
A robber ducky!

When I came across that big pile of free pants on the street, I really picked up the slack.

I was going to buy some thin sandals to wear on my beach trip.
But then I flip-flopped.

What did the kid say when his math teacher gave him a yardstick?
"This rules!"

Why did Miss Muffet need a map?
Because she lost her whey.

The kid's pants zipper broke.
But he fixed it on the fly.

What's round and angry?
A vicious circle.

I didn't want to know that she had false teeth, but some things come out in conversation.

What do brooms say to each other at bedtime?
"Sweep tight!"

What's another name for a grandfather clock?
An old-timer.

What did the big bucket say to the little bucket?
"You look a little pail."

Why did the teddy bear turn down dessert?
Because he was stuffed.

A beautiful marble statue decided to move off of
her perch. She was tired of being taken for granite.

Where does a power cord go shopping?
The outlet mall.

You should read this book about how boats are held together.
It was riveting.

A man went into a hardware store and asked to see some tools he could use to break up hard ground. The clerk took him to a wall of shovels, hoes, and other tools.
He says, "Take your pick."

The teacher quit their job teaching kids how to do origami. Too much paperwork.

My mom gave some old rope a time-out.

It was being very knotty.

Have you heard the joke about the roof?

Never mind, it's definitely over your head.

Did you hear the one about the unstamped letter?

Never mind, you won't get it.

What vitamin will sting you?
Vitamin B.

Want to hear a joke about paper?

Never mind, it's tearable.

Two houses situated next door to each other fell in love.

It was a lawn-distance relationship.

A nickel and a penny jumped off a moving train together.

But not the quarter. It had more cents.

"This job isn't for everyone," the scarecrow said, "but hay, it's in my jeans."

I call my alarm "Jim."
That way I can tell people the first thing I do every morning is hit the Jim.

"Boy," said one shelf to the other shelf, "you sure look board."

Your fingers are a lot like the hardware store.
They've both got a lot of nails.

How do "Stop," "Merge," and "Yield" signs communicate?
Sign language.

Telling puns in an elevator is just wrong on so many levels.

Where do boats go when they get sick?
To the dock.

You can have my chimney for free.
It's on the house!

Why did the beams get together once a week?
It was their support group.

Did you hear that metal and a microwave fell in love?

When they met, sparks flew!

I asked my friend, Nick, if he had 5 cents I could borrow.

But he was Nicholas.

I bought a wooden whistle . . . but it wooden whistle.

What kind of shoes do ninjas wear?
Sneakers!

He couldn't work out how to fix the washing machine.

So he threw in the towel.

If you buy a bigger bed you actually get less bedroom.

These reverse-angle cameras in cars are great.

I got one and I never looked back.

The candle quit its job.

He felt burned out.

If you 're looking for a rugged experience,
try traveling on a flying carpet.

My phone has to wear glasses.
Well, ever since it lost its contacts.

People say I look better without my glasses on.
But I just can't see it.

If artists wear Sketchers . . . then do linguists wear Converse?

I just read a book on anti-gravity.
I couldn't put it down!

My new diet consists entirely of aircraft.

It's a bit plane.

Why are there fences on graveyards?

Because people are dying to get in.

Remember: Models of dragons are not to scale.

I owe a lot to the sidewalks.

They've kept me off the streets for years.

How do you keep an ig from falling off?

Igloo.

Towels can't tell jokes.

They have a very dry sense of humor.

I thought this old rope would be useful, but nope—a frayed knot.

Never trust an escalator.

They're always up to something!

That poor piece of paper pinned up to the wall!

It was under a tack.

Why did the smelter get arrested?
For steeling the iron.

There's nothing more odd than numbers not divisible by two.

Do houses wear clothes?
Sure—a dress.

What do you call a belt with a watch on it?
A waist of time.

A broken can opener is really just a can't opener.

I'm sorry you got hit on my way into the room.
Honestly, I a-door you.

A woman came home to find she'd been robbed of every lamp in her house.
She was de-lighted.

Never leave your wooden shoes in the bathroom. Otherwise people will think you clogged the toilet.

A man was walking through a quarry when he remarked, "Wow, what a big rock."

"Boulder," his friend said.

So he replied,

"Oh my goodness that's the MOST AMAZING ROCK I'VE EVER SEEN!"

There's a wash basin standing in front of your door right now.

Just let that sink in.

They could make pencils with erasers on both ends. But then, what would be the point?

Him: Does it seem weird that there's just one big factory that makes all the perfume in the world?

Her: Yeah, it makes scents.

Not only is a bride's last name new, she also gets a dress.

That table was so rude.

It said it couldn't chair less!

A girl brought a ladder to the first day of classes.

She thought she was starting high school.

How do you stop a baby spaceship from crying?

Rocket.

A belt was recently arrested.

It was caught holding up a pair of pants.

The mama toilet let her kid stay home from school one day.

She was looking a little flushed.

What did the hat say to the scarf?

"You can just hang around. I'll go on a head."

Never was there a more groundbreaking invention than the shovel.

Two of my friends always liked to sit right by the window.
Classic Kurt and Rod!

How come a bicycle can't stand up on its own?
It would, but it's two-tired.

Eating a clock may seem like a good idea, but keep in mind that it's very time consuming.

Have you picked up one of those brand-new state-of-the-art brooms?

Well, they're sweeping the nation!

I got a bump on my head because a book fell on it.

Sure, it hurts, but really, I only have my shelf to blame.

Two smartphones got married.

The wedding was a simple affair, but the reception was excellent.

What did one shirt say to the other?
"Meet me at the clothesline. It's where I hang out."

Did you hear about the guy who got a universal remote control?

He just held it in his hands and said, "This changes everything!"

One wind turbine met another wind turbine the other day and was very excited.

"What can I say?" it said. "I'm a big fan!"

Did you hear about the hungry clock?

It went back four seconds.

Person: "You ate the dictionary? Bad dog! Spit it up."
Dog: "You took the words right out of my mouth."

Girl: I used to have a terrible fear of hurdles.
Boy: What did you do?
Girl: I got over it.

The thing about whiteboards is that they're remarkable.

Did you hear about the girl who lost her watch?
She wanted to find it, but she didn't have the time.

I asked a tailor to make me a brand-new pair of pants.
He was happy to do it, or sew it seems.

Did you hear about the electronics shop downtown that's giving out dead batteries?
Yep, totally free of charge.

This one goes out to the guy who invented zero.
Thanks for nothing!

I got into the car the other day and I seemed to have forgotten how to buckle my seatbelt.
I struggled for a while until finally it clicked.

I really want to buy one of those new reversible jackets.
I'm excited to see how it turns out.

For some reason, my best friend left a ton of clay at my house.
I don't know what to make of it.

How do you make an hourglass run faster?
Fill it with quicksand.

If you have wrinkled clothing, it's certainly a pressing issue.
You'll need to iron out a solution.

This small sweater fits great, but it is hard to pull off.

Of all the jobs out there, being a mirror inspector is one I could really see myself doing.

Would you like to check out my mind-reading machine?
I'd love to hear your thoughts.

A guy walks into a restaurant and orders a meal.
He hears someone say,
"Hey, guy! Nice pants! Nice shirt! Great jacket!
Where did you get those amazing shoes?"
He looks around and realizes that there's nobody else around.
The waiter comes over and points to the bread basket.
"It's the rolls," he says. "They're complimentary."

I ordered a book of puns last week.
But I didn't get it.

12
VERY TECHNICAL—Computers, Gadgets, etc.

Why was the computer so nervous?

It couldn't get with the program.

Why did the doctor keep checking his TV?

To see if it was operational.

Why didn't the nut like the bolt?

Because he was screwed up.

How do clouds communicate?

They Sky-pe!

How did the bed learn to play piano?

Using sheet music.

What do you call it when a computer gets new shoes?

Rebooted.

What did the computer say when the salesperson asked if they could help?

I'm just browsing.

What happened to the light when the switch was feeling down?

It couldn't go on.

Why did the barn fall down?

It wasn't stable.

Why didn't the computer
know what to do?

It lost its "memory"

Why were there so many lines between the words?

They were spaced out.

How did the dog get its data back?

It retrieved it.

Why do birds make the best scientists?

They already have their own beakers.

Why did the pen write a circle around the word joke?

It was just joking around.

What is a straw's favorite flower?

Two lips.

How do knights change their TV channels?

With a remoat.

Why was the screw so mad?

Because it didn't get its turn.

Where did the computer and the Internet go when they went out?

On a data.

When do movies do what they are told?

On demand.

Why wouldn't the PC talk about its problems?

It was too personal.

Where does the computer's cat like to sleep?

On its lap-top!

What happens if you give the king of the jungle an Xbox?

You get a lion gamer.

How did the computer monitor describe the keyboard?

Kind of touchy.

How will bees get their packages delivered in the future?

By drones.

Why don't phones wear glasses?

They have contacts.

What is something you should never do to your headphones?

Poke them in their iPhone.

Why was the computer sneezing?

It had a virus!

LOAD VIRUS 60Z

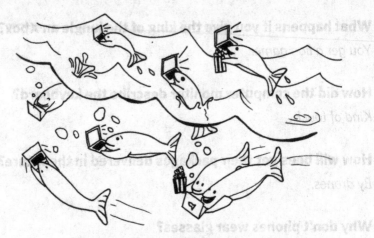

How were the fish able to watch
the latest movie?

They were streaming it!

Why did the coin machine
feel guilty?

Because it broke
a dollar!

What do romantic Twitterers say?

Tweet nothings!

What did the computer do after taking a big breath?
It ex-celled.

How did the smartphone get smarter?
It studied its text books.

How can a phone take pictures without anyone else pushing a button?
All by its selfie.

Why did the chicken want a GPS?
To help it get to the other side of the road.

What do you call a phone that won't share?
Cellfish.

What's an astronaut's favorite
Key on the computer?

The space bar!

What kind of underwear
do lawyers wear?

Legal
briefs!

What did one app say to the other app about going on the computer?

Icon if I want to!

Why was the computer always happy?

It had a really good Outlook.

Why did it take so long for the laptop to get in the door?

It was trying all of its keys.

What did the computer ask the tech?

How about you get with the program?

How do candles get together on the Web?

They use their wikis.

Why did the stove always get mad?

It was hot-tempered!

What is a shark's favorite type of technology?
Bluetooth.

How did the fence share its favorite moments?
By posting them.

How did the disc put on its makeup?
It used its compact.

What do you get when you cross a battery and a zombie?
A battery that will never die.

How do clocks communicate?
They tick-tock to each other.

What video game do pigs like to play in the car?

Wii wii wii all the way home!

Why did the pens decide to become friends?
They just clicked.

Why did the computer set a trap?
It had a mouse.

What did the e-mail tell the document?
All good things come to a send!

How did one mouse feel about the other mouse finding the cheese?
It was amazed.

What did the speakers say to the TV that made it nervous?
You're surrounded!

How do you know a computer needs glasses?

It has trouble seeing the sites!

How do trees sign off of their computers?

They log out.

How would you talk to Santa if he were a computer?

You would sit on his laptop.

Which fish did the computer pick for a pet?

The betta.

Why did the exterminator have to spray the computer?

He had to debug it.

Why did the computer like tennis?

It was a good server.

Why did the smoke detector have to go?

It wasn't very alert.

What did the projector say as its bulb was being replaced?

But the show must go on.

What do you call it when a picture goes to the mall?

Photo shopping.

What is a computer's favorite part of art class?

The cutting and pasting.

Why did the sand turn into glass?

It wanted to make a spectacle of itself.

Why did the notebook need glasses?

It couldn't read between the lines!

Why couldn't anyone get the computer open?
It was all locked up.

Why don't bugs need cable to watch TV?
They have their own antennas.

What was the sports camera's only dream?
To go pro.

Why was the money off by itself in the bank?
It was all a-loan.

Where do TV's like to go on vacation?
To remote places.

Why was the corn so good at music?

It could play by ear.

What do you do with an upset Web site?

You com it down.

How can a computer see the world?

Through its Windows.

How does a clock put its gloves on?

One hand at a time.

Why didn't the toys want to go to the party?

The batteries weren't included.

What does a witch use to make sure her hex will work?

Spell check!

How did the caveman let his friends
know what he was doing?

He posted it on his wall!

Why does every pair of pants look different?

They all have different genes.

Why was the clock so mad at the marker?

It had written all over its face.

What did the recorder tell the microphone?

You can say that again.

What did the Web site ask the mouse?

Can you take me home?

How do you know when a balloon comes in unannounced?

When it bursts into the room.

Why did the piggy bank need to be fixed?

It was broke!

How do you know when your screwdriver is sick?

It takes a turn for the worse.

How did the Instagram account know someone was there?

They were following him.

Where does the world's biggest spider live?

In the World Wide Web.

How do birds communicate?

They tweet.

Why did someone keep dropping the flash drives?

They were all thumbs.

What do you get when you
cross earphones and a flower?

Ear buds!

What do you get when you combine a cow with the Internet?

Some milk and a bunch of cookies.

How does a DVD player get from place to place?

It lets the disc drive.

What is the fastest cracker in the box?

An Instagraham.

Where do e-mails like to play?

In their sent box.

What do you feed your big screen?

A TV dinner.

13
ON THE JOB—Work, Jobs, etc.

When you're named dentist of the year, they give you a reward. It's just a little plaque.

Did you hear about the woman who used to be a train driver?
She got sidetracked.

Never trust an acupuncturist.
First they needle you, and then they end up stabbing you in the back!

Can I fill you in on my trip to the dentist?

My molars are really bothering me. Good thing I have a dentist appointment today.
At 2:30.

Santa's best toy-making elf left the North Pole and started her own very successful toy company.
Now she's extremely welfy.

Receptionist: Hello, please take a seat. The dentist will see you shortly.
Patient: Thank you, I'm familiar with the drill.

After the police caught the burglar, they poured cement on the culprit.

Now he's a hardened criminal.

Did you hear about the singer who got locked out of her house?

She broke into song and couldn't find the key.

After he quit pirating, the peg-legged pirate got a job waiting tables. At IHOP.

My grandfather is a baker, but he's never let me have his gingerbread recipe.

He said it's on a knead-to-know basis.

Did you hear about the pirate who covered his eye with sandpaper?

He was in a bit of a rough patch.

Pirates have a hard time getting through the alphabet.

They always get lost at C.

What did the pirate say when his wooden leg fell off during a snowstorm? "Shiver me timbers!"

Why didn't the pirate take a bath before he walked the plank?

Because he figured he'd wash up on shore later.

"Yarr," said one pirate to another,
"what a nice wooden peg ye got thar. . . .
And such a shiny hook, too! How much did they cost?"

The other pirate said, "An arm and a leg."

What's another name for a happy cowboy?
A jolly rancher!

What did the pirate say on his 80th birthday?

"Aye matey!"

Old carpenters don't retire.

They just lumber around.

If you're ever searching for a job, the trick is to look inside yourself.

Then, it's all about the inner view.

Did you hear about the skeleton comedian?
It was trying tibia little humerus.

What's the most tedious place in an office?

The bored room.

The pilot liked to be alone.

But even for him, flying a drone was just too remote.

What car would a farmer drive?

A cornvertible.

The failed poet decided to leave the writing to the prose.

What do you call a carnivore who also forecasts weather? A meat-eorologist.

We hired a tree trimmer and he did a great job.

He should take a bough!

What happened when the worker rotated the heavy machinery?

He got cranky.

I got fired from my job flipping burgers.

Apparently I didn't turn up enough.

After years of hard work on the subject, the excited scientist finally unlocked the secret to human cloning. He was beside himself!

My brother got a job making telescopes.

Things are looking up!

Did you hear about the barista who quit her job at the coffee shop?

She couldn't stand the daily grind.

I was supposed to do a list of odd jobs.

I finished numbers 1, 3, 5, 7, and 9.

I used to work as a hairdresser,
but I just wasn't cut out for it.

A witch published a book of all her potion recipes, but it was ultimately useless.

She'd forgotten to run a spell-check.

When construction workers party, they raise the roof!

The ship's captain was expected to dock in a very tiny little space. . . .

He was under a lot of pier pressure.

Why did the scarecrow get promoted?
Because he was outstanding in his field.

We hired a door-maker the other day.

She really knew how to make an entrance.

My new girlfriend tends to bees all day.

She's a keeper!

The fishing company had a very catchy slogan:

"Yes, we can!"

A man sued an airline company after it lost his luggage.

Unfortunately, he lost his case.

Why did the man dig a hole in his neighbor's backyard
and fill it with water? He meant well.

I was accused of being a plagiarist.

Their words, not mine.

The "old woman who lived in a shoe" wasn't the sole owner.

There were strings attached.

A persistent banker wouldn't stop bothering me.

So I asked him to leave me a loan.

I hear that the post office is a mail-dominated industry.

What does a fisherman magician say?
"Pick a cod, any cod!"

A doctor broke his leg while auditioning for a play.

Luckily, he still made the cast.

The balloon maker had to close down her business.

She couldn't keep up with inflation.

Government leaders don't engage in surfing contests. . . .

It could set a president.

Kid: How do you like your job?
Garbage Collector: It's picking up.

Electricians are the friendliest people on the planet.
They really know how to make good connections.

Why are kindergarten teachers so great?

They know how to make the little things count.

A scientist wanted to clone a deer.

So he bought a doe-it-yourself kit.

A man was fired from his job at the calendar factory.

Just because he took a couple of days off!

Barbers are excellent drivers.

They know all the shortcuts.

Why couldn't the lifeguard rescue the hippie?
He was too far out, man.

A ship carrying red paint shipwrecked.
It marooned all the sailors.

I know a tailor who doesn't mind making a pair of pants for me.
Or sew it seams.

I used to be a banker.
Until I lost interest.

Did you hear about the psychic with four heads?
They were a real four-chin teller.

Kitchen remodelers are very counterproductive.

A man heard that gold was discovered in Alaska. He immediately packed up his possessions and moved up there. Six months later, he gave up and went home.
It didn't pan out.

They buried the man in the wrong place.
Talk about a grave mistake.

Doctors are monitoring the condition of the boy who swallowed a handful of pennies, to see if he's passed them. No change yet.

This one police station lets criminals take their own pictures. They call them cellfies.

How come the detective stayed in bed all day?
She was working undercover.

Patient: Doctor, my nose is running.
Doctor: I think it's not.

How do dog catchers get paid?
By the pound.

What do you call a student who always turns in their math homework late?
A calcu-later.

When the medieval warrior was awarded by the king, he was given a knighthood.
It was a big sir prize!

Policeman: Got any I.D.?
Lady: Got any I.D. about what?

How are actors going out on stage like little kids?
They like going to the play-ground.

I just produced a theatrical performance on puns.
It was a play on words.

14
WILD KINGDOM—Knock Knocks About Animals

Knock knock! *Who's there?*
Udder. *Udder who?*
Would you like to hear an udder knock-knock joke?

Knock knock! *Who's there?*
Achilles. *Achilles who?*
Achilles mosquitos if they don't quit biting me!

Knock knock! *Who's there?*
Mike Howell. *Mike Howell who?*
Mike Howell give you lots of milk!

Knock knock! *Who's there?*
Arnold. *Arnold who?*
Arnold dog can't learn new tricks!

Knock knock! *Who's there?*
Conch. *Conch who?*
Conch you come outside for a while?

Knock knock! *Who's there?*
Lionel. *Lionel who?*
Lionel bite you if you get too close at the zoo!

  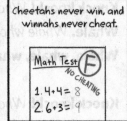

Knock knock! *Who's there?*
Distinct. *Distinct who?*
Distinct of de skunk out here is de worst!

Knock knock! *Who's there?*
Gibbon. *Gibbon who?*
Why are you Gibbon me such a hard time?

Knock knock! *Who's there?*
Polly Warner. *Polly Warner who?*
Polly Warner cracker?

Knock knock! *Who's there?*
Whale. *Whale who?*
Whale, whale, whale, what have we here?

Knock knock! *Who's there?*
Sham. *Sham who?*
Sham-u, the killer whale!

Knock knock! *Who's there?*
Kelp. *Kelp who?*
Kelp me get a gift for my mom.

Knock knock! *Who's there?*
Fido. *Fido who?*
Fido away, will you miss me?

Knock knock! *Who's there?*
Rabbit. *Rabbit who?*
Rabbit up and let's go!

Knock knock! *Who's there?*
Quacker. *Quacker who?*
Quacker 'nother bad joke and I'm outta here!

Knock knock! *Who's there?*
Flea. *Flea who?*
Flea blind mice, flea blind mice, see how they run, see how they run . . .

Knock knock! *Who's there?*
Oink-oink. *Oink-oink who?*
Are you a pig or an owl?

Knock knock! *Who's there?*
Ocelot. *Ocelot who?*
Ocelot of questions, don't you?

Knock knock! *Who's there?*
Dog. *Dog who?*
Dog-gone it, open the door!

Knock knock! *Who's there?*
Cows go. *Cows go who?*
No, cows go moo.

Knock knock! *Who's there?*
Amoeba. *Amoeba who?*
Amoeba silly, but I really like knock-knock jokes!

Knock knock! *Who's there?*
Dino. *Dino who?*
Dino-mite!

Knock knock! *Who's there?*
Spider. *Spider who?*
Spider what everyone says, I like you!

Knock knock! *Who's there?*
Newt. *Newt who?*
Newt to this neighborhood, can you show me around?

Knock knock! *Who's there?*
Viper. *Viper who?*
Viper nose, it's running!

Knock knock! *Who's there?*
Honeybee. *Honeybee who?*
Honeybee a dear, and go get me a soda.

Knock knock! *Who's there?*
Geese. *Geese who?*
Geese what I'm going to do if you don't open the door!

Knock knock! *Who's there?*
Tick. *Tick who?*
Is tock there? It's time we got back together!

Knock knock! *Who's there?*
Baby owl. *Baby owl who?*
Baby owl see you around sometime?

Knock knock! *Who's there?*
Panther. *Panther who?*
Panther what you wear on your legths.

Knock knock! *Who's there?*
Robin. *Robin who?*
Robin your house!

Knock knock! *Who's there?*
Meow. *Meow who?*
Take meow to the ball game . . .

Knock knock! *Who's there?*
Feline. *Feline who?*
Feline fine, thanks for asking! You?

Knock knock! *Who's there?*
Moose. *Moose who?*
Moose you always be so suspicious?

Knock knock! *Who's there?*
Gnats. *Gnats who?*
Gnats not funny!

Knock knock! *Who's there?*
Weevil. *Weevil who?*
Weevil stay just a minute, promise!

Knock knock! *Who's there?*
Beehive. *Beehive who?*
Beehive yourself!

Knock knock! *Who's there?*
Stork. *Stork who?*
Stork up on food—storm's a comin'!

Knock knock! *Who's there?*
Ostrich. *Ostrich who?*
Ostrich my arms up to the sky!

Knock knock! *Who's there?*
Toucan. *Toucan who?*
Well, toucan play that game!

Knock knock! *Who's there?*
Giraffe. *Giraffe who?*
Giraffe anything to eat in there?

Knock knock! *Who's there?*
Heron. *Heron who?*
Heron any knock-knock jokes you like yet?

Knock knock! *Who's there?*
Bee. *Bee who?*
Bee yourself!

Knock knock! *Who's there?*
Badger. *Badger who?*
I'll badger no more if you let me in!

Knock knock! *Who's there?*
Elephant. *Elephant who?*
You forgot to feed the elephant!

Knock knock! *Who's there?*
Bat. *Bat who?*
Bat you'll let me in soon.

Knock knock! *Who's there?*
Fur. *Fur who?*
Waiting fur you to open the door.

Knock knock! *Who's there?*
Chimp. *Chimp who?*
I think it's pronounced shampoo.

Knock knock! *Who's there?*
Pooch. *Pooch who?*
Pooch your arms around me, baby!

Knock knock! *Who's there?*
Claws. *Claws who?*
Claws the door behind you.

Knock knock! *Who's there?*
Possum. *Possum who?*
Possum food to me, I'm hungry!

Knock knock! *Who's there?*
A herd. *A herd who?*
A herd you were home so I came right over.

Knock knock! *Who's there?*
Beaver. *Beaver who?*
Beaver quiet, and no one will hear us!

Knock knock! *Who's there?*
Kanga. *Kanga who?*
No, kangaroo!

Knock knock! *Who's there?*
Hee-haw. *Hee-haw who?*
Well, are you a donkey or an owl?

Knock knock! *Who's there?*
Koala. *Koala who?*
Koala the cops, I've been robbed!

Knock knock! *Who's there?*
Collie. *Collie who?*
Collie-flower is good for you.

Knock knock! *Who's there?*
Mustang. *Mustang who?*
Mustang up the phone and answer the door!

Knock knock! *Who's there?*
Safari. *Safari who?*
Safari so good.

Knock knock! *Who's there?*
Anteater. *Anteater who?*
Anteater dinner, but Uncle wasn't hungry.

Knock knock! *Who's there?*
Weasel. *Weasel who?*
Weasel while you work . . .

Knock knock! *Who's there?*
Otter. *Otter who?*
You otter apologize to me!

Knock knock! *Who's there?*
Howl. *Howl who?*
Howl you know . . . unless you open the door?

Knock knock! *Who's there?*
I lecture. *I lecture who?*
I lecture dog out of the yard, sorry!

Knock knock! *Who's there?*
Wood ant. *Wood ant who?*
Don't be afraid, I wood ant hurt a fly!

Knock knock! *Who's there?*
Cat. *Cat who?*
Cat you think of a better joke than that?

Knock knock! *Who's there?*
Cattle. *Cattle who?*
Cattle purr if you pet her.

Knock knock! *Who's there?*
Goose. *Goose who?*
Goose see a doctor for that cough!

Knock knock! *Who's there?*
Rhino. *Rhino who?*
Rhino every single knock-knock joke!

15
WHEN A FART ISN'T A FART—
Toots, Farts, Gas, etc.

What do ninjas and farts have in common?

They are both silent and deadly.

Why did the conductor fart so loud?

He wanted to toot his own horn.

What do you call passing gas in a pair of borrowed pants?

A fart transplant.

Why do teenagers fart so much?

Because it is the only gas they can afford.

What do you call a person who is too shy to fart in public?

A private tooter.

Q: *Why don't farts graduate from high school?*
A: *Because they always end up getting expelled.*

How can you tell if a person has a good imagination?

They think their farts smell good.

What is the stinkiest country?

Fargentina.

What do a bowl of chili and a filling station have in common?

They both give you gas.

What can go right through your pants and not leave a hole?

A fart.

The Flamingo: A fart so substantial that you have to stand on one leg to help it get out.

The Organ Grinder: That rare fart that comes out in multiple tones that it sounds like you're playing a jaunty, old-timey tune.

TYPES OF FARTS

Farts come in all shapes and sizes. Have you ever experienced any of these?

• **The Crescendo:** *A fart that starts quiet . . . but that just keeps getting LOUDER.*

• **The Déjà vu:** *When you swear you've smelled something just like it before, somewhere, sometime.*

• **The Trapper Keeper:** *The hostile act of a fart in an enclosed space, like a compact car or an elevator.*

• **The Zombie:** *When a fart smells so nasty that you're sure you're dead and are slowly rotting from the inside out.*

• **The Rapid Fire:** *A bunch of farts all at once that make a rat-tat-tat-tat-tat sound, like you're a machine gunner on a warship.*

• **The Odorless Wonder:** *A fart that's all noise and no smell, but still somehow just as embarrassing.*

• **Flavor Country:** *A fart so nasty that you don't just smell it, but you taste it a little, too.*

• **The Bubbler:** *A fart sneakily emitted in a bathtub or hot tub that just looks like a bigger bubble.*

• **The Whodunit:** *A silent but stinky fart in a crowded place . . . but only you know who was responsible. (It was you!)*

• **The Drowned Out:** *A fart let loose in a place so loud—a concert, a sporting event, a dance club—that nobody knows you did it.*

• The Forgiven: *A fart in church that nobody is going to call you out for.*

• The Mosquito Bite: *A fart that hurts just a little bit.*

• The Fair Warning: *It may feel, sound, and smell like a simple fart, but you understand it for what it is: a two-minute warning to get to the bathroom . . . and fast.*

Where do ghost farts come from?
Booooooooooties.

Did you hear about the guy that ate an entire bowl of baked beans before going to the ballet?

He shouldn't have.

Did you hear about the girl that was in love with the smell of her own farts?

She was inflatuated.

What's the difference between the
Mona Lisa and passing gas?

One is a work of art. One is a work of fart.

Did you hear about the couple that were perfect for each other?

She was a heartbreaker and he was a fart-breaker.

How can a fart surprise you?

If it's got a lump in it.

What do you call a group of superheroes after a chili competition?

The fartastic four.

If you're an odious gas, life begins at farty.

Why does a black hole never fart?

Because nothing can escape it!

Where's the best place to buy beans?

At the gas station.

Where do farts go skating?

At the roller stink.

What do you call a fart you make in the laundry room?

A fluffy.

Did you hear about the prince who ate too many beans?

It resulted in noble gas.

Did you hear about the fart joke book?
It was a best smeller!

What do you call a baby's fart?

Little stinker.

Did you hear about the incident at the bean factory?

There was a gas leak.

How many teenagers does it take to stink up a room?

Only a phew.

Did you hear about the fart factory that not only made farts but also sold them?

Their motto was, "Whoever smelt it, dealt it."

What University smells the worst?

P.U.

Did you hear about the grandma that ate too much broccoli?

She was an old fart.

How does a cow's fart smell?

Udderly terrible.

A fart is just a poop . . .

• *that doesn't believe in itself.*

• *that's honking for your butthole to get out of the way.*

• *calling to let you know he's running late.*

• *sounding the evacuation alarm.*

What's the stinkiest piece of clothing?
A windbreaker.

Did you hear about the boy who couldn't stop farting in class?

He was a-gassed!

What do you call a Mozart fart?

Classical gas.

What smells worse? A burp or a fart?

Hard to say, but together they could knock out a horse.

What did the brave man do?

Took a chance on a fart after a day of diarrhea.

Why do farts smell so bad?

So your deaf Grandpa can enjoy them too!

Why shouldn't you fart in an Apple store?

They don't have Windows.

Why won't vampires feast on weathermen?

They give them wind.

How do you know it's time to go to the bathroom?

When the coffee cup's empty.

What did the astronaut say before he farted?
Blast off!

What do you call a vegan with diarrhea?
A salad shooter.

How do you make still water turn to sparkling?
Easy, just fart in the glass!

I didn't fart. That was just my bowels blowing you a kiss!

Why was the surfer scared to go into the water?
Farts were circling.

Why was the RV so stinky?
Because it was full of gas.

License to Smell

Some people love bathroom humor so much they have to take it on the road!

• *LUV2FRT*

• *IFRTID*

• *IGOTTAP*

• *RNONGAS*

- *KSMYGAS*

- *OLDFRT*

- *PASNGAS*

- *ICUP*

- *LUVSHARTZ*

- *BUTKISR*

- *STOLBUS*

- *TURDLE*

- *DIDUFRT*

- *NVRFLSH*

- *BGDMP*

- *EATMCRP*

- *EATMGAS*

- *H8FARTS*

- *GOT2POO*

- *JCYPOO*

What do stinky kids eat for breakfast?
Pooptarts.

John: *What's the best way to catch a fart?*
Lou: *Why would anyone want to catch a fart?*

TOP 5 BEST PLACES TO FART

- *Walking past first-class boarding a plane.*

- *In the library next to a rude person who is being too loud.*

- *In an elevator if you were riding with someone who didn't return a hello.*

- *When someone cuts in line behind you.*

- *In your coach's office. After you've just been cut from the team.*

Why did Pocahontas eat a bag of fruity jelly beans and then fart?

Because she wanted to paint with all the colors of the wind.

What did the lady with a run in her stockings do?

She got to a bathroom, quick!

Why can you only put 359 beans in a soup?

Because one more would make it "Too Farty!"

Want to know an easy way to transform your tub into a jacuzzi?

Take a bath after eating broccoli casserole.

Did you hear about the lost fart?
He turned into a burp.

Why did the teenager finally quit farting?
He ran out of gas.

What is rude, can travel through solid material, and can bring you to tears?
Farts.

Sunday	Monday	Tootsday	Wednesday	Thursday	Friday	Saturday
3	4	5	6	7	8	9

What is the stinkiest day of the week?
Tootsday.

Did you hear about the fart that went on an adventure?
It made a great escape!

Why did the woman pass gas in the elevator?
She wanted to take her farts to a new level.

Why did the boy fart in the cemetery?
Because he read a tombstone that said RIP.

How did the ninja hide his fart?
He masked it.

Why are farts so wholesome?
Because it's what's on the inside that counts.

Did you hear about the kid who just turned 10 and ate too much prune cake?
He turned his birthday party into a birthday farty.

In space, no one can hear you fart . . . and if you're wearing a spacesuit, only you can smell it.

What causes cold winter winds?
Frosty, after eating a bowl of chili.

What's green and smells like flies?

Kermit's farts.

What do you get when you fart in a shepherd's pie?

Never invited over for dinner again.

Little Johnny: *Mom! Dad! I was the only kid that knew the answer to the question the teacher asked today!*
Mom: *That's wonderful! What was the question?*
Little Johnny: *Who farted?*

What kind of pizza smells like farts?

Smell-eroni pizza.

What happens when you cross an atomic bomb with beans?

A weapon of gas destruction!

Have you heard about the new line of Fartphones?

I wouldn't buy one. They're real stinkers.

Did you hear about the bad student with bad gas?

He kept getting farter behind, so his parents hired him a tooter.

Why can't farts get a decent education?

Because they always get expelled.

16
THE WHOLE STORY—
Literary Jokes, etc.

Did the godmother use her wand in time?

Yes, she was fairy fast!

Why did Pinocchio ask so many questions?
He was very nosey.

What do you call a poem you can say over and over again?
A reverse.

What do you get when you combine a rock with a newspaper?
Hard times.

What did Humpty Dumpty do after the fall?

He went to pieces.

What happened after Jack broke his crown?

It all sort of went downhill from there.

Why did Thomas get in trouble at the table?

For chugging down his drink.

What do all of the storybook characters think of Red Riding Hood?

She's cape-able.

What did the Three Little Pigs say when there was no one at the door?

Werewolf?

How long did it take to get rid of the dragon?

Two Knights!

Why couldn't Cinderella play baseball?

She was always running away from the ball!

How do clocks start their bedtime stories?
Once upon a time . . .

When did the king ask for the royal joker?
Jest in time.

Which storybook character could be an author?
Little Red Writing Hood.

What did one story say to the other?
You're telling me!

What do you have when you have two ducks and a goose?
A game!

Who did little Miss Peep invite to the dance?

Her Bo!

What did Miss Muffet say when
the spider asked for her curds?

No Whey!

What did the mirror say to the Queen when Snow White won?

You need to face it.

What did Jack say the second time he went down the hill?

I'm not falling for that again!

How come Jack can never be king?

Because he broke his crown.

Where do you keep a wild squash?

In a zoochini.

How did Alice finally figure out where she was?

She put on her looking glasses.

Why can't the three bears ever open the door?

Goldie locks it!

Why was Baa Baa always getting into trouble?

Because he was the black sheep of the family.

How do you find a book in a hospital?

You page it.

What's the last thing an author will ever write?

The end.

Why wouldn't the artist read the cartoon novel?

It was too graphic.

Why was the story so mad at the writer?

He was plotting against it.

Why did the book go to the chiropractor?

To have its spine adjusted!

What were Baby Buntings first and last words?

Bye-Bye.

Why was the whole Miss Muffet thing such a drama?

It was an itsy bitsy spider.

Where did Peter Peter's wife go?

The pumpkin eater.

How did the pirate know it was time for tea?

Polly Put the Kettle On.

Why was Wee Willie winking?

He had something in his eye.

Why were the flowers so smart?

The roses are read to.

Why was Simon so mad?

Someone called him simple.

When do kings worry the most?

When the reign stops.

How did the book feel about its beginnings?

Fairly contents.

How can you tell when a nursery rhyme is ready for bed?

It's Wynken, Blynken, and Nodding.

How come Briar Rose was so pretty?

She got a lot of beauty sleep!

Why didn't Hansel and Gretel follow the trail?

It was too crumby!

What did the pans say when the vegetable's story grew longer?

Asparagus the details and go on.

Why wouldn't the porridge go outside in the summer?

It was too hot.

What did the spider say when Miss Muffet finished all of her curds?

Whey to go!

How did the pie get Little Jack to talk about what the thumb had done to it?

It cornered him.

How much garbage did the black sheep have?

Three bags full.

How did the book talk to its friends?

By text.

Why was the library book so detached?

It checked out.

Why was the book first in the race?

It was bound to win.

Why were the words and spaces agreeing?

They were on the same page.

What happened when the giraffe wrote a book?

It's a long story.

How did the monster feel about being green?

It had to get ogre it!

What did Juliet say when she climbed into the boat?

Row-me-o!

Why couldn't the story stay at the hotel?

It was all booked up.

What did the frog say to the tadpole?

I froget what were we doing?

Where did the story go?

It booked it out of here.

What did Little Bo have to say about the lost sheep?

Not a peep.

How did the fairy tale end?

It was kind of Grimm.

What does Pinocchio get when he blows his nose?

Splinters!

What did Little Boy Blew?
His nose.

What did the gardener say that made everyone think he was color blind?
Lavender's blue.

What nursery rhyme is never told in the desert?
Rain Rain Go Away

What did Prince Charming and Cinderella do at the dance?
They had a ball.

What sound did Peter Piper make when he was little?
A Pitter patter.

How do chickens have such nice eyebrows?

They pluck them.

How is Cinderella always prepared for sports?

She's wearing a ball gown.

How did everyone learn that Wilbur was some pig?

On Charlotte's Web site.

What is most attracted to Iron Man?

Magnets.

Where do the magicians play when they're kids?

In magic tree houses.

Why did Humpty Dumpty crack up?

Someone pushed him over the Edge

How did the Hatter find the whole Alice dilemma?

Maddening!

Why was the giant so excited?

It was his big day!

Why wouldn't Rapunzel come out of her room?

She was having a bad hair day!

Where do spies get their flowers?

In a secret garden.

How much cheese does the Wimpy Kid like on his sandwich?

Just a touch.

What do ghosts hate to drive through?

Phantom tollbooths.

What did one yellow creature say to the other yellow creature after he did him a favor?

Thanks a minion.

What do silly birds write in?

Stork Diaries.

How do you know when a wolf
doesn't have a winning hand in cards?

He huffs when he bluffs!

Which snicket is the most sour?

Lemony Snicket.

Where does the street start?

Where the sidewalk ends.

What did the stools say when they got on the bus?

Don't Let the Pigeon Drive.

What do you call it when you play sports on an empty stomach?

Hunger Games.

Who stole everyone's thunder?

The lightning thief.

What kind of net was stuck
to the Knight in shining armor?

A magnet!

What did the spider say to her new friend?

Hi, Fly Guy.

Which superhero is a lousy boxer?

Captain Underpants.

How did everyone know the book was happy?

It had a big Smile.

How did Rapunzel and her hair feel about each other?

They never wanted to be a part.

What bear is the biggest complainer?

Whiny The Pooh

Which storybook character could be an author?

Little Red Writing Hood!

What was the scared baby goat's favorite book?

Diary of a Wimpy Kid.

How did Spider Man meet Spider Woman?

On the Web.

Who was the biggest king in history?

King Kong.

How did Captain Underpants get so strong?

He used to be a boxer.

17
THE SPORTS SECTION—
Athletes, Sports, Games, etc.

How do archers get in shape?
They do arrowbics!

Golfers always wear two pairs of pants when they're out on the links.

Just in case they get a hole in one.

Boxers have a very dangerous job. They constantly put themselves in arm's way.

Race car drivers are often very hungry.

It's because they skip brake fast.

With the way they use those wooden bats, baseball players are really just lumber-jocks.

What do you call it when two wrestlers join forces?

A clobberation.

When does a baseball game start?

In the big inning.

A lot of people think Rafael Nadal is a really good tennis player, but isn't Roger Federer?

What's the difference between a baseball player and a dog?

The baseball player gets a whole uniform. The dog only pants.

What do football stars and waffles have in common?

They're both made on the gridiron.

I used to know this really funny joke about a boomerang.

I forgot it, but I'm sure it will come back to me.

What basketball player smells the best?
The scenter!

The outdoors store was filled to the brim with people during its big paddle sale.
It was quite the oar deal.

A sports arena is a great place to spend a hot day.
It's full of fans.

That race car driver has had a very checkered past.

What kind of tea do hockey players drink?
Penal-tea.

Why are soccer players so good at math?

They know how to use their heads.

What do hockey players and magicians have in common?

Hat tricks!

What's a runner's favorite class?

Jog-raphy!

Where do tennis players like to live?

Volleywood!

Bungee jumping is an expensive sport.
Like they say, there's no such thing as a free lunge.

Why did the basketball player sit on the court and draw pictures of chickens?

She was trying to draw fowls.

What time did the basketball team chase the baseball team?

Five after nine.

Why is basketball so gross?

All the dribbling!

I didn't think I was going to like fencing, until I decided to take a stab at it.

I didn't think I was going to like soccer,

but as it turns out, I really get a kick out of it.

What do golfers wear on the links?

Tee-shirts.

If you're out camping and get cold, never build a fire in a kayak.

You can't have your kayak and heat it, too.

Skydivers chute first, ask questions later.

It's no wonder they're so well-grounded.

Why did the ballerina quit?
Because it was tutu hard.

Baseball is a team effort, especially those in the bullpen.

Everybody has to pitch inning.

People who do scuba.

Now there's a divers group of individuals.

I tried archery, but I didn't like it.

There were too many drawbacks.

A longshot was leading the big horse race, but not furlong.

Did you hear about the extremely indecisive rower?
He couldn't pick either oar.

A fishing pole is really just a fish stick.

How did the baseball player lose his house?

He made a home run.

When the coach called in a new pitcher, it was such a relief.

Have you ever thrown a spitball?

No, and I hope to never get invited to one either!

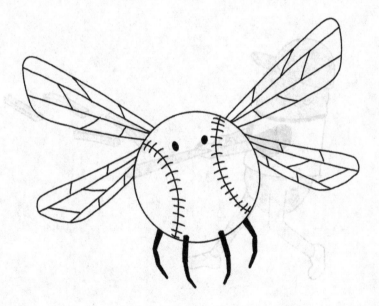

What do you get when insects play baseball?
Fly balls.

Why do they play baseball games at night?

Because bats sleep during the day.

What's the first thing that a ball does when it stops rolling?

It looks round.

First kid: Why is our tennis teacher so mad at you?

Second kid: He caught me raising a racquet.

What do you get when potatoes play baseball?
Fry balls.

What time does Serena Williams wake up each day?

Oh, ten-ish.

The bowling pins were tired of being mistreated.

So they went on strike.

What's the best time of year for jumping on a trampoline?

Spring!

Did you hear about the pig that joined the baseball team? She played snortstop.

We were going to tell you a joke about swimming, but it was too watered down.

Why shouldn't you ever play basketball with pigs?
Because they're ball hogs.

Cinderella was terrible at sports.
Probably because her coach was a pumpkin.

Did you hear about the ghost that joined the soccer team? It played ghoultender.

Cinderella was terrible at soccer.

She kept running away from the ball.

Do you want to hear a story about a basketball player?

It's a tall tale.

What did the football coach say to the broken vending machine?

"Give me my quarterback!"

Why are fish such terrible basketball players?
They're afraid of the net!

What got the martial artist so sick?

Kung flu.

Why didn't the dog like to wrestle?

Because she was a boxer.

A fish was arrested for swimming without a license. Police caught him and let him go.

That's when the fish said, "Whew, I'm off the hook!"

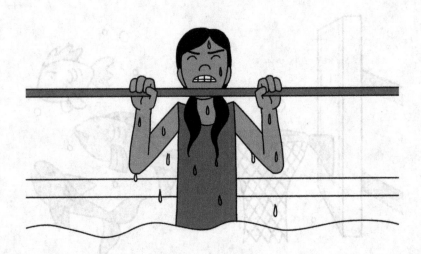

What exercise do swimmers do to get strong?
Pool-ups.

What's the difference between a baseball hit really high and a maggot's dad?

One's a pop fly, the other is a fly's pop.

What would you call a female goaltender standing between the two goal posts?

Annette.

What's the difference between a fisherman and a bad student?

One baits his hooks, the other hates his books.

Why are archers the best dressed of all the athletes?
They're always sporting bow ties.

Actual Names That Real People Have Given Their Boats

Vitamin Sea

Yacht to Be Working

Fah Get a Boat It

Costa Lotta

Seas the Day

Breakin' Wind

Your Place Oar Mine

A Crewed Interest

Bow Movement

Sea Me Smile

My Pride and Toy

Rest a Shore

Docked Wages

Seize the Bay

Fishfull Thinking

Weather Oar Knot

Nuclear Fishin'

Why did the athlete want to buy nine racquets?

Cause tennis too many.

A really bad gymnast walked into a bar.

Volleyball players can always make extra money.

It's customary to tip a good server.

What's a banker's favorite track and field event?

The vault.

On the bus on the way to the meet, the track team never stopped talking.

I guess they had a lot to discus.

How come sun tanning never caught on as a competitive sport?

Because the best you can ever get is bronze.

Yes, I'm competing in that stair-climbing competition.
Guess I better step up my game.

I lift weights only on Saturday and Sunday.
Monday to Friday are weak days.

Lately, my skiing skills are really going downhill.

A fisherman tried boxing, but he only threw hooks.

I think there are about two million or so baseball diamonds in the world.
But that's just a ballpark figure.

I know a lot of jokes about bad pole-vaulters.
But none of them seem to go over very well.

After hours of waiting for the bowling alley to open, we finally got the ball rolling.

I was overruled at the measuring competition.

The athlete claimed he long-jumped over 25 feet. Actually his best jump only measured 23 feet.

This was a clear case of leap fraud.

Him: . . . and that's how they invented hockey.
Her: Icy.

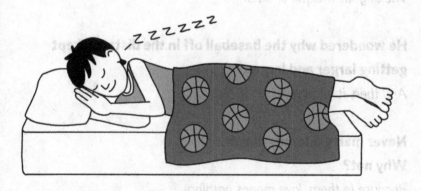

Basketball players are always so well-rested.
You see, taller people sleep longer.

Did you hear about the Olympic speed skaters who refused to spend much money on their equipment?

Such cheapskates!

What's an NBA player's favorite TV drama?

The Mentallest.

You can't always be a Winter Olympics champion.

You win some, you luge some.

Did you hear they had to close down the ballpark because of an animal infestation?

The dugout was full of bats.

He wondered why the baseball off in the distance kept getting larger and larger.

And then, it hit him.

Never marry a tennis player.
Why not?

Because to them, love means nothing.

What's a boxer's favorite part of a joke?

The punchline!

18
THE "OBJECT" OF LAUGHTER—Knock Knocks About Objects

Knock knock! *Who's there?*
Shoes. *Shoes who?*
Shoes me to come in there, and not anybody else!

Knock knock! *Who's there?*
Stopper. *Stopper who?*
Stopper, she just ran away with your newspaper!

Knock, knock! *Who's there?*
Accordion. *Accordion who?*
Accordion to the weather forecaster, it's going to rain tomorrow.

Knock knock! *Who's there?*
Statue. *Statue who?*
Statue? This is me.

Knock knock! *Who's there?*
Aisle. *Aisle who?*
Aisle see you around!

Knock knock! *Who's there?*
Jewel. *Jewel who?*
Jewel be sorry!

Knock knock! *Who's there?*
Freighter. *Freighter who?*
Freighter snakes? I know I am!

Knock knock! *Who's there?*
Adopt. *Adopt who?*
Adopt my pencil on the ground and it rolled away.

Knock knock! *Who's there?*
Thistle. *Thistle who?*
Thistle make you laugh!

Knock knock! *Who's there?*
Diesel. *Diesel who?*
Diesel man, he played one . . .

Knock knock! *Who's there?*
Swatter. *Swatter who?*
Swatter you doing later?

Knock knock! *Who's there?*
Iota. *Iota who?*
Iota leave!

Knock knock! *Who's there?*
York hat. *York hat who?*
York hat kept me up all night caterwauling!

Knock knock! *Who's there?*
Hair. *Hair who?*
Hair today, gone tomorrow!

Knock knock! *Who's there?*
Issue. *Issue who?*
Issue crazy? It's me!

Knock knock! *Who's there?*
Heart. *Heart who?*
Heart you glad to see me?

Knock knock! *Who's there?*
Knee. *Knee who?*
Knee-d you ask?

Knock knock! *Who's there?*
Icon. *Icon who?*
Icon tell you a different knock-knock joke if you like.

Knock knock! *Who's there?*
Diploma. *Diploma who?*
Diploma is here to fix de sink!

Knock knock! *Who's there?*
Fiddle. *Fiddle who?*
Fiddle make you happy, I guess I'll tell you.

Knock knock! *Who's there?*
Razor. *Razor who?*
Razor hands in the air like you just don't care!

Knock knock! *Who's there?*
Train. *Train who?*
Someone needs to train you to answer the door when people knock!

Knock knock! *Who's there?*
Mustache. *Mustache who?*
Please let me in, I mustache you an important question!

Knock knock! *Who's there?*
Bingo. *Bingo who?*
Bingo-ing to come see you for ages!

Knock knock! *Who's there?*
Chess. *Chess who?*
Me!

Knock knock! *Who's there?*
Tennis. *Tennis who?*
Tennis too many dogs for this small house!

Knock knock! *Who's there?*
Tide. *Tide who?*
Tide of these knock-knock jokes yet?

Knock knock! *Who's there?*
Ice. *Ice who?*
Ice to see you, too.

Knock knock! *Who's there?*
Eyes. *Eyes who?*
Eyes better come in before it gets too dark.

Knock knock! *Who's there?*
Rain. *Rain who?*
Rain, dear, like the ones that pull Santa's sleigh!

Knock knock! *Who's there?*
Weed. *Weed who?*
Weed better leave soon.

Knock knock! *Who's there?*
Ear. *Ear who?*
Ear you are, at long last!

Knock knock! *Who's there?*
Cargo. *Cargo who?*
Cargo "beep-beep!"

Knock knock! *Who's there?*
Radio. *Radio who?*
Radio not, here I come!

Knock knock! *Who's there?*
Dumbbell. *Dumbbell who?*
Dumbbell doesn't work so I had to knock!

Knock knock! *Who's there?*
Window. *Window who?*
Window you think we'll get tired of these knock-knock jokes?

Knock knock! *Who's there?*
Nose. *Nose who?*
I nose a lot more knock-knock jokes, if you're interested in hearing them.

Knock knock! *Who's there?*
Sonata. *Sonata who?*
Sonata big deal.

Knock knock! *Who's there?*
Comet. *Comet who?*
Comet a crime, and you'll go to prison.

Knock knock! *Who's there?*
Clothesline. *Clothesline who?*
Clothesline all over the floor are going to end up wrinkled.

Knock knock! *Who's there?*
Detail. *Detail who?*
Detail of de cat is on de end.

Knock knock! *Who's there?*
Atlas. *Atlas who?*
Atlas, you're home!

Knock knock! *Who's there?*
Stopwatch. *Stopwatch who?*
Stopwatch you're doing and open up!

Knock knock! *Who's there?*
Botany. *Botany who?*
Botany good books lately?

Knock knock! *Who's there?*
Dishwasher. *Dishwasher who?*
Dishwasher way I spoke before I got my dentures.

Knock knock! *Who's there?*
Acid. *Acid who?*
Acid down and be quiet!

Knock knock! *Who's there?*
Thermos. *Thermos who?*
Thermos be a better knock-knock joke than this one!

Knock knock! *Who's there?*
Cotton. *Cotton who?*
Cotton a trap. Help me get out!

Knock knock! *Who's there?*
Dots. *Dots who?*
Dots for me to know, and you to find out!

Knock knock! *Who's there?*
Ooze. *Ooze who?*
Ooze been telling you all these terrible knock-knock jokes?

Knock knock! *Who's there?*
Wooden shoe. *Wooden shoe who?*
Wooden shoe like to be my neighbor?

Knock knock! *Who's there?*
Bug spray. *Bug spray who?*
Bug spray that spiders won't eat them!

Knock knock! *Who's there?*
Saber. *Saber who?*
Saber, she's drowning!

Knock knock! *Who's there?*
Disguise. *Disguise who?*
Disguise de limit!

Knock knock! *Who's there?*
Wheel. *Wheel who?*
Wheel stop telling these jokes when we're good and ready!

Knock knock! *Who's there?*
Cadillac. *Cadillac who?*
Cadillac mad if you step on his tail.

Knock knock! *Who's there?*
Auto. *Auto who?*
Auto know, but I forgot.

Knock knock! *Who's there?*
Snow. *Snow who?*
This is snow time for questions, open up. It's snowing!

Knock knock! *Who's there?*
Dozen. *Dozen who?*
Dozen anybody wanna come out and play?

Knock knock! *Who's there?*
Hatch. *Hatch who?*
Have you got a cold or something?

Knock knock! *Who's there?*
Tire. *Tire who?*
Tire shoelaces or you'll trip and fall!

Knock knock! *Who's there?*
Nuisance. *Nuisance who?*
What's nuisance the last time I saw you?

Knock knock! *Who's there?*
Husk. *Husk who?*
Bless you!

Knock knock! *Who's there?*
Ore. *Ore who?*
Ore else!

Knock knock! *Who's there?*
Brick. *Brick who?*
Brick or treat!

Knock knock! *Who's there?*
Gunpowder. *Gunpowder who?*
Gunpowder my nose.

Knock knock! *Who's there?*
Stick. *Stick who?*
Stick around.

Knock knock! *Who's there?*
Armor. *Armor who?*
Armor friends in there?

Knock knock! *Who's there?*

Chest. *Chest who?*

Chest got back from vacation!

Knock knock! *Who's there?*

Arrow. *Arrow who?*

Arrow on the side of caution.

Knock knock! *Who's there?*

Oak. *Oak who?*

Oak out below!

Knock knock! *Who's there?*

Wool. *Wool who?*

Wool you let me in?

Knock knock! *Who's there?*
A boat. *A boat who?*
A boat time I got here.

Knock knock! *Who's there?*
Kimono. *Kimono who?*
Kimono my house sometime!

Knock knock! *Who's there?*
Zipper. *Zipper who?*
Zipper-dee-doo-dah!

Knock knock! *Who's there?*
Canoe. *Canoe who?*
Canoe *please* get off my foot?

Knock knock! *Who's there?*
Lavender. *Lavender who?*
Lavender world laughs with you.

Knock knock! *Who's there?*
Cologne. *Cologne who?*
Cologne Ranger!

Knock knock! *Who's there?*
Dew. *Dew who?*
Dew something about your room, it's a mess!

Knock knock!

Who's there?

Tree.

Tree who?

Tree more days until vacation!

19
BUTT, WHY?—Bums, Rear Ends, Keisters, etc.

What soda do butts like best?

Squirt.

Why are only the cleanest butts allowed to sing solos?

Because they are soap-ranos.

What do you call an old butt that has seen it all?

A wise crack.

Where do butts buy their groceries?

Hole Foods.

What do butts and lasers have in common?

They both go "pew-pew"!

What music band do butts like best?

Tom Petty and the Fart Breakers.

What is the grossest reality show?

Shart Tank.

What do butts eat at the movies?

Poopcorn.

What's the worst thing someone
can do in the bathroom?

Mix up the toilet brush for a toothbrush.

What's another name for panda poop?

Endangered feces.

What do you get when you put a turd in the freezer?

A poopsicle.

What do you get after eating too much ice cream?

A chocolate swirl.

What did the guy get when he couldn't make it to the bathroom in time?

Heavy pants.

What's the worst thing you can do in the laundry room?

Mistake the dryer for a toilet.

What basketball team can't control their bowels?

The San Antonio Spurts.

How many logs can you fit in an empty toilet?

One. After that, it isn't empty anymore.

Why did the pastry chef use jalapeños?

He wanted to ensure his buns were hot.

What did one fireman say to the other in the bathroom?

Fire in the hole!

What's worse than finding a fly in your soup?

Finding a fly in your poop.

What do you get after eating too many Oreos?

Cookie dookie.

Why was the mathematician's bowel movement so upsetting?

Because it had a lot of problems.

What did the boss hang up in the bathroom for the employees to read?

A list of do's and doo doos.

Did you hear this book is a #2 bestseller?

Why was the ditch digger so constipated?
He was a mud clutcher.

What was the constipated librarian doing in the bathroom?
Working on the backlog.

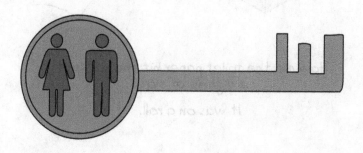

What do you use to unlock the bathroom door?
A doo-key.

What did the comedian say when he looked at his poop?

Yuk yuk.

How did the toilet paper hit the jackpot
in a game of slots?

It was on a roll.

When is the most satisfying time to go to the bathroom?

Poo thirty!

Where is the most painful place to go number two on a car trip?

A fork in the road.

What do you get after eating too many blueberries?
Smurf poop.

What place did the piece of poop get in the race?
Turd place.

What do you never appreciate until it's gone?
Toilet paper.

What's brown, sticky, and sounds like a clock tower?
Dung.

How do you get your butt to wipe itself?
Eat toilet paper.

How is a butt like the Liberty Bell?
They both have a big crack.

What happens after you eat too much alphabet soup?
You get really bad vowel movements.

When is laughter the worst medicine?
When you have diarrhea.

What is another name for Eskimo poop?
Pudding-pops.

FOUL LANGUAGE

Believe it or not, these are real quotes—because even the most interesting people in history love to talk about what we do in the bathroom.

"Everybody looks at their poop."
—Oprah Winfrey

"Always go to the bathroom when you have a chance."
—King George V

"Home is where the heart is, home is where the fart is."
—Ernest Hemingway

"Fart for freedom, fart for liberty—and fart proudly."
—Benjamin Franklin

"An employer's fart is music to his employees' ears."
—Mokokoma Mokhonoana

"You failed—your fart was not silent, my nose heard its deafening noise."
—Aniekee Tochukwu Ezekiel

"My trumpeting sounds like a goose farting in the fog."
—Alex O'Loughlin

"You are all made of real poop."
—Anne Frank

"Men who consistently leave the toilet seat up secretly want women to get up to go to the bathroom in the middle of the night and fall in."
—Rita Rudner

What's worse than a big juicy fart coming out of your butt?
A big juicy fart going into your butt.

What do you call a poop that comes out really sloooooooow?
A turdle.

What did the guy say after he made a square poop?
"Ouch."

Why did the cook wipe his butt before he pooped?
He liked to make things from scratch.

fahrvergnügen: A German word that means "driving pleasure."

fahfrompüpen A German word for constipation.

What's the one thing in the world that feels even better than being in love?

Finding a clean toilet when you're out in public when diarrhea strikes.

What do a spaceship and toilet paper have in common?

They both probe Uranus.

What's the easiest way to lose two pounds?

Drop off a deuce in the bathroom.

How was the boy able to fart so loudly that it fell on a thousand ears?

He did it in a cornfield.

What did the surfer say in the bathroom?

Wipe out!

Why did the clarinet player smell so bad?

She was always practicing her wind instrument.

Why did the secretary stay in the bathroom for so long?

Because no job is finished until the paperwork is done.

A little boy in church needed to go to the bathroom. "Mom, can I go take a dump?" he asked. "Yes," his mother replied, "but we're in church. Next time don't say 'dump,' say 'whisper.' It's more polite." The next Sunday, the boy is sitting by his father, and again he needed to use the bathroom. "Dad, I have to whisper," the boy said. "Okay," the father replied. "Whisper in my ear."

I tried to follow Constipation on Twitter, but got blocked.

Why did the man poop on his lawn?

He was too cheap to buy fertilizer.

Why did the salesman poop in the furniture store?

Because the customer asked to see a stool sample.

What's another name for a poop that floats?

Bob.

Why did the woman put plastic wrap
on the toilet seat?

She wanted to seal in the freshness.

Why did the King stay on his throne?

He was constipated.

What do you do when you find blue poop in the toilet?

Try to cheer it up.

Did you hear about the author who couldn't poop for a week?

Talk about a bad case of writer's block.

Where does the government keep all the most valuable farts?

Fart Knox.

What's the most unpopular activity at summer camp?

Farts and Crafts.

Why are farts worse than bad breath?

Because you can at least put a mint in your mouth.

What's a toilet's favorite kind of frozen yogurt?

Chocolate swirl.

What does an umpire say after he takes a poop?

"You're out!"

What does the lifeguard say after he goes to the bathroom?

"Everybody out of the pool!"

POO-PHEMISMS

• *Coaching the Browns*

• *Dropping the lobster in the water*

• *Drowning a rat*

• *Feeding the porcelain puppy*

• *Cutting bait*

• *Freeing the hostages*

• *Making mud pies*

• *Putting the meat loaf in the oven*

• *Logging on*

• *Letting some air out of the tires*

- *Making a doo-posit*

- *Baking brownies*

- *Crowning a new king of Brownland*

- *Checking in on breakfast*

- *I got an anaconda who don't wanna be in my buns, hon*

- *Wink at the toilet for an extended period of time*

- *Back that thang up*

- *Baiting the trap*

- *Bombing the porcelain sea*

- *Helping the beavers build a dam*

- *Going to play Call of Doody*

What soda tastes like prunes?

Dr. Pooper.

Have you seen *Howard's End*?

You probably shouldn't. That's where his poop comes from!

Did you hear M. Night Shyamalan directed a movie about an impacted colon?

There was a twist at the end.

What is the stinkiest palindrome?

POOP.

What's worse than finding fake poop in your bed?

Finding real poop in your bed.

Did you hear about the guy who desperately stumbled into the bathroom in the middle of the night and couldn't find the toilet?

It was a shart in the dark.

Why did the dad only change his baby's diaper one time?

The box said up to 20 pounds.

A 60-year-old, a 70-year-old, and an 80-year-old were all playing bingo when the 60-year-old said, "Being 60 is the worst age. I sit on the toilet all day and I can't pee at all!"

"That's nothing," said the 70-year-old. "I can't even poop!"

"No," said the 80-year-old. "I have the worst age."

"Do you have trouble peeing?" the 60-year-old asked.

"No, not at all. Every day at 6 a.m."

"What about pooping?" the 70-year-old asked.

"Not a problem. 6:30 a.m.," he said.

"So you're telling me," the 70-year-old said, "that you have the hardest age, but you can pee and poop easily? What's the problem?"

"The problem is that I don't get up till 8 o'clock."

How is your younger sibling like a diaper?

They're always full of it, and always on your butt.

What did the rectum say was its relationship status on Facebook?

"It's constipated."

What's green, hairy, has three legs and smells horrible?

I don't know either. But I found it in the toilet!

Why shouldn't you buy shampoo?
It's fake. Get real poo.

Bill: How do you define messy?

John: Dirty and unorganized?

Bill: No, the bathroom after you get done with it!

What did the worried mom leave in the toilet?

A nervous wreck.

Bill: Did you have corn for lunch?

John: Yes, how did you know?

Bill: You forgot to flush the toilet.

What do you call a supermodel with a bad case of diarrhea?

A hot mess.

What happens after you eat peppers?

They get jalapeño dirty business.

Did you hear about the basketball player who had diarrhea?

He got called out for double-dribbling.

What flower do you give someone
who overcomes constipation?

A ploppie!

What did the toilet say on *Wheel of Fortune*?

I'd like to buy a bowel, please!

Did you hear about the guy who posted online every time he pooped?

He had a log blog.

Did you hear about the man who didn't poop for months and then got diarrhea?

Talk about a blast from the past.

Did you hear about the high school kid who pooped out a misshapen log in total silence?

It was a teenage mutant ninja turdle.

Police: *Sir, please open the door and come out immediately.*

Man: *But I'm pooping!*

Police: *Yes, but you're in a taxi.*

Did you hear about the new album by the band Diarrhea?

It leaked early.

Which Pokémon can't control its bowels?

Squirtle.

What kind of pants can you poop in?
Dungarees.

What happens if you eat too many Mexican jumping beans?

Your poop will jump right out of the toilet.

On which carnival ride is it okay to poop your pants?

The dumper cars.

What's brown and spins around your waist?

A hula poop.

20
EARTH DAZE—Nature, The World, Living Things, etc.

A's are a lot like flowers.
Bees follow them.

Did you hear about the belly button?

It was so smart that it went to school at the Navel Academy.

Did you hear the joke about the virus?

Never mind, I don't want to spread it around.

What's unthinkable?

An itheberg.

What part of a flower can power a bicycle?
The petals.

Why do trees make such terrible enemies?

Because they're the best at throwing shade!

Do you want a brief explanation of an acorn?

It's an oak tree, in a nutshell.

First Kid: Did you know that I can cut down a dead tree just by looking at it?

Second Kid: I know. I saw it with my own eyes!

The campfire was nearly dying, but now it's roaring again. "I'm stoked!" the fire said.

What month do trees dread?

Sep-timber!

Take it from a scientist:

Never believe atoms. They make up everything.

The tree was very successful.

So much so that it opened up lots of branches.

The trees were more than glad when fall and winter had both passed.

In fact, they were re-leafed.

What did the trees wear to the forest pool party?
Swimming trunks.

There's no real way to tell if someone is color-blind.
There's a lot of gray area.

I'd tell you a chemistry joke, but I know I wouldn't get a reaction.

Groups of really intelligent trees tend to grow next to each other.
It's called a brainforest.

If you think it's bad when it's raining cats and dogs, you should try hailing taxis.

What kind of trees do you get when you plant kisses?
Tulips.

What did the right eye say to the left eye?

"Between you and me, something smells."

They had a funeral for some boiled water.

It will be mist.

The clouds in the sky got so excited that it was spring that they wet their plants!

What's the best way to start a fire?

That's a subject that has been hotly debated.

Two flowers decided to grow next to each other.
After all, they were buds!

No two people interpret colors the exact same way.

In fact, it's a pigment of your imagination.

Some astronomers were supposed to watch the moon rotate for 24 whole hours.

But then they got bored and called it a day.

How do trees access the internet?

They log on.

There's nothing like a meteor shower
to rock your world.

During the middle of a heat wave, our town got dumped with snow.

The weatherman says it was an ice-olated incident.

The earth's rotation really makes my day.

Only one large petal remained on the old rose.

Last bud not least!

Why did the tonsils get all dressed up?
Because they heard a doctor was taking
them out tonight!

Why are trees such big sports fans?

They just like to root!

What did the cowboy say when the varmint gave him flowers?

"What in carnation?"

Gardeners hate weeds.

That's because if you give them an inch, they'll take a yard.

How do florists make money?

By petaling their goods.

How do big mountains in cold areas stay warm in the winter? Because they're topped with snowcaps.

Why didn't the scientist give her mother flowers on her birthday?

She hadn't botany!

What's the top prize at a flower show?

A bloom ribbon!

I now know how gemstones are made.

The process is crystal clear!

Gardeners love their work.
Going to their job everyday is like a bed of roses!

Trees hate taking tests.

Those questions always stump them!

Trees are living things, and they get sleepy, too.

They occasionally need a nap—forest.

The nose was feeling very sad.

It was so tired of getting picked on.

People using umbrellas always seem
to be under the weather.

There was a big natural disaster the other day.

The earthquake took the blame, saying "it was my fault."

Why did the piece of coal turn into a diamond?

It just couldn't take the pressure.

Why do geologists like their area of study so much?

It rocks!

In order for a fungus to grow, you have to give it as mushroom as possible.

A lot of people have big noses, but a nose cannot be longer than 12 inches. If it was, it would be a foot.

If you want to make some money, get into flower sales.

Business is blooming!

Most people prefer the summer to the winter.

And yet, snow happens weather you like it or not.

How do meteorologists greet each other?

With a heat wave!

There's only one tree that can fit in your hand.
A palm tree.

How do clouds salute the president?

They hail to the chief!

The weather forecast called for freezing rain today.

And sure enough, it was an ice day.

Do you think plant puns are funny?

We're fern believers!

The moon saves money by cutting its own hair.
How? Eclipse it.

During allergy season, it's best to wake up early and get all that snot out of your nose at once.
Sneeze the day!

Never discuss infinity with a mathematician.
They can go on about it forever.

What's the best way to impress an orchid?
Use lots of flowery language.

How come the little kid's tooth fell out?
Because it was looth.

If you live in an igloo, there's snow place like home.

21
YOU'RE HISTORY—Olden Days, Ancient Stuff, etc.

The only American president
who was both a licensed barber and
a former professional wrestler: Abraham Lincoln.

President James Garfield was an ambidextrous genius.
He could write in Latin with one hand and in Greek with
the other . . . at the same time!
Write on, man!

Borrow a dollar?
**The most valuable piece of money ever issued
in the U.S. was a $100,000 bill.** It was only
printed from 1934 to 1935.

Today, the largest bill in circulation is the $100 bill.
In 1969, the U.S. government got rid of all banknotes
worth more than that.
So, did they just throw them away?

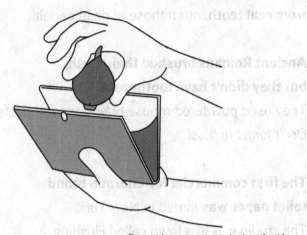

Got change for a flower? In the 1630s, tulip bulbs could be used as currency in Holland. The value varied greatly: at its peak, a single tulip could be traded for an entire estate. But when its value crashed, one tulip was the price of an onion.

George Washington didn't have wooden teeth.
He had four sets of dentures (fake teeth), and they were made from elephant ivory, hippo bone, and human teeth, held together with golden springs. *Wood sounds better, actually.*

Washington was lucky!
Dentures have been made for centuries.
Up until the 1800s, they were **usually made**

from real teeth, often those of dead people.

**Ancient Romans brushed their teeth,
but they didn't have toothpaste.**
They used powdered mouse brains as toothpaste.
Don't forget to floss!

**The first commercial for Charmin brand
toilet paper was** filmed in New York.
The studio was in a town called Flushing.
Makes perfect sense.

Just like "Yankee Doodle."
**In the 1700s, "macaroni" was a slang term
that meant "fashionable man."** It's an Italian word,
and Italy was thought to have the most
stylish people.

Out of this world!
**Cleopatra's lifespan was closer to the time of the
first moon landing** (in 1969 A.D.) than to the time
the Great Pyramid of Egypt was built (around 2560 B.C.).

While Cleopatra ruled in ancient Egypt, she often wore a fake beard in public. Well, she was de queen of denial!

The world's first commercial communication satellite was *Intelsat I*. It was launched in 1965, and it's still in orbit.
Space is the place!

Only one time has a satellite been wrecked by a passing meteor. A space rock killed the European Space Agency's *Olympus* in 1993.
Olympus has fallen!

Not enough hours in the day?
The speed of the Earth's rotation changes over time.
A day in dinosaur times was only 23 hours long.

The Canadian province of Nova Scotia doesn't want to displace historical artifacts. It's illegal to scavenge with a metal detector there, with a fine of $10,000. *Do not disturb!*

Pharaoh-really?
Think all of the pyramids are in Egypt? Wrong—**there are more pyramids in Sudan than in Egypt.**

What's in a name?
West Virginia split off from Virginia in 1863. It was almost named Kanawha, after an indigenous tribe.

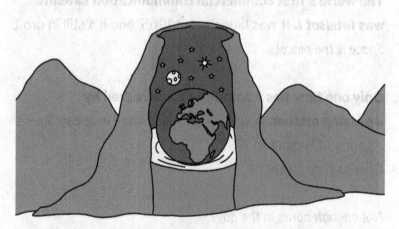

Ancient Babylonians thought that the Earth wasn't round but inside a hollow mountain, floating on a giant ocean. The sun, moon, sky, and stars were also inside the mountain. Hey, at least they didn't think it was flat.

Roll call!

Who was that Native American woman notable for her association with the colonial settlement at Jamestown, Virginia? **Pocahontas was just her nickname.** Her real name, given by her people, was Matoaka.

The original Bluebeard?
Archaeologists say the Great Sphinx of Egypt at one time had a red face and a blue beard. (It's faded over the years.)

A very attractive bit of trivia.

The ancient Greek philosopher Thales thought that magnets had souls. He figured that since they attracted and repelled each other, they were sort of alive.

Yeti is another name for Bigfoot.
In 1959, the U.S. government gave its embassy in the
Asian country of Nepal a list of guidelines for how to
safely hunt the Yeti there. They haven't found
one yet-i.

When he died, Chinese emperor Qin Shi Huangdi
(who ruled from 259 B.C to 210 B.C.) **wanted his body
to be safe in case he ever came back to life**. So he
had his tomb surrounded by 8,000 clay soldiers,
130 clay chariots, and 670 clay horses.
He still hasn't woken up.

When mummies were made in ancient Egypt,
the brain had to be removed.
Mummy makers pulled it out through a nostril.
Next time you blow your nose, yell, "Brains!"

Archaeologists have found honey in the tombs of ancient Egyptian pharaohs. It was still edible.

So that means they tasted it?! Eww!

What's all the buzz?
In ancient Egypt, **slaves were ordered to smear themselves with honey** and stand near the pharaoh. Their job: to keep flies away from him.

President Ronald Reagan personally saved the lives of 77 people. When he was a young man, he worked as a lifeguard.

And they probably all voted for him.

Look at all the baby presidents!
What was it about the year 1946? During a 66-day period, future presidents Bill Clinton, George W. Bush, and Donald Trump were all born.

President Andrew Johnson was a self-taught tailor.
He made clothes both for himself and for his
closest political advisors.
The clothes make the man!

The White Zoo?
Past presidents had some pretty unusual pets.
Calvin Coolidge's animals included raccoons, a pygmy
hippo, and lion cubs. Herbert Hoover's son owned a pair
of alligators.
Teddy Roosevelt's family included a lizard, a pig, a bear,
and a one-legged rooster.

Not an Eagles fan.
Founding Father Benjamin Franklin didn't want the
eagle to be the national symbol of the United States.
He preferred the turkey.

In the 1860s, the state of Maryland had such a problem with boats from Virginia invading their shorelines to fish for oysters that the government formed an official "oyster navy" to defend the beaches. Was not sharing those oysters shellfish?

Time to moove out . . .
William Taft's cow, Pauline, was **the last cow to live at the White House**. She provided milk for him during his presidency.

The grand wooden desk in the Oval Office is made out of repurposed wood. It used to be part of an old U.S. Navy ship.
How a-boat that?

You're never too young . . . or old.
In 1975, 43-year-old **Donald Rumsfeld was appointed Secretary of Defense as the youngest person ever to hold the position**. In 2001, 68-year-old Rumsfeld was again appointed Secretary of Defense, and was the oldest person ever to hold the position.

Welcome to the jungle.
Navy SEALs are some of the most highly skilled and elite troops in the world. **When SEALs served in the Vietnam War, they wore pantyhose,** because it kept off the leeches that live in the jungle.

Strike a pose . . . **How statues of war heroes are posed reveals a lot about the person.** If they're on a horse that has both front legs in the air, the person died in battle. If the horse has one front leg in the air, they died of wounds received in battle. If the horse has all four legs planted, the person died of natural causes.

King Alfonso IX ruled León (it's now part of France) from 1188 to 1230. When leading his troops, he'd get so riled up that he'd drool uncontrollably and foam at the mouth. That's why **he was known as Alfonso the Slobberer.**
You've got a little something on your face, your majesty.

How long did the **Hundred Years' War** between England and France last? **Not 100 years—it took place from 1337 to 1453.**

Then why not call it the 116 Years' War?

Go, Joe!
There was a "real American hero" named G.I. Joe.
He was a carrier pigeon during World War II.

Gotta have that morning pick-me-up.

The most popular way to drink coffee in Italy is as a small cup of highly concentrated and caffeinated espresso. **During World War II, Italian soldiers stationed in North Africa carried their own individual espresso makers.**

Bacon bombs away!

During World War II, the American Fat Salvage Committee collected donated bacon fat from homes. It was used to make glycerin, which was used to make bombs.

The oldest alarm system:
Ancient Romans guarded their homes with guard dogs.
They even displayed "beware of dog" signs – whether there were dogs on the property or not.

It's unknown who actually invented the fire hydrant. There was a patent . . . but it was destroyed in a fire.

If only they'd had a fire hydrant!

Everybody has to start somewhere.

Before he founded Microsoft, Bill Gates's first business was a company called Traf-O-Data. It automatically recorded the number of cars driving on streets.

The first cell phones were released in 1983. The Motorola DynaTAC 8000x weighed four pounds and cost $4,000.

And you couldn't even use Instagram on it.

They're not just into teeth.

The electric chair was invented by a dentist. So was cotton candy.

She just did it.

The Nike logo—the "Swoosh"—was designed by a college student named Carolyn Davidson. She was paid $35 at the time, but Nike later gave her more than $600,000 worth of free shoes.

Faster! Faster!
The first roller coaster in America opened
at Coney Island in New York in 1884. Known
as a switchback railway, it was invented by
LaMarcus Thompson and inspired by contraptions
used to move coal. The coaster traveled only
six miles per hour.

In the present-day world of the Internet, **humans
collectively generate more data in two days than
was created in all of history** up until the year 2003.
That's a lot of Snaps!

A powerful fact.
**There's more computing power
in a smartphone than there was in the computers
that sent man to the moon.** All of NASA's computers
combined couldn't match what's in the average person's
pocket.

When he visited France in the 1700s, **Thomas Jefferson
snuck some rice seeds into his pockets and smuggled
them back home.** That was highly illegal—if he'd been
caught, he might have been put to death.
No, no, no, Mr. President!

Graffiti—art or messages drawn on a public building without permission—isn't a modern thing. **Archaeologists found graffiti on a wall dating to first-century Rome** that read "Successus was here."
Classic Successus!

Sure, Thomas Jefferson wrote the Declaration of Independence. But did you Know that he also invented the swivel chair? Wheeeeeee!

Where there's a Will, there's a way.
During his lifetime, **Shakespeare's last name was spelled 83 different ways.**

Pull up your [BEEEEP!]
In 19th-century England, **"pants" was considered a very dirty word.**

Anyone have an eraser? Pennsylvania is spelled "Pensylvania" on the Liberty Bell. At the time, this spelling was one of several acceptable spellings for the state.

Not everybody wants to be president.
In 1952 Albert Einstein was offered the presidency of Israel. He turned down the offer.

Join the party!

For more than 150 years, every American president has been either a Republican or a Democrat.
The last president who wasn't was Millard Fillmore, a member of the Whig Party, who left office in 1853.

We're sure there's a scientific explanation for this. Albert Einstein made a lot of breakthroughs in science, but he always had cold feet. Einstein never wore socks.

Swinging from two branches!

William Howard Taft was president of the United States from 1909 to 1913. After he left office, he later got to hold his actual dream job: Chief Justice of the Supreme Court. **Taft is the only person to serve as both president and Chief Justice.**

Grover Cleveland is the only president to serve two terms not in a row, and **he's the only president who had an artificial jaw.** In 1893, he needed to have part of his jaw removed because of a tumor, and it was replaced with one made of rubber.
Bionic president!

Get a leg up.
"Shanks" are another name for legs. **King Edward I of England (he ruled from 1272 to 1307) had such long legs** that his nickname was Longshanks.

A speedy recovery.
In 1947, test pilot **Chuck Yeager got his plane up to 767 mph, breaking the sound barrier.**
Two days earlier, he broke two ribs when he fell off a horse.

Merrily, merrily, merrily . . . In 1968 and 1969, **a British man named Robin Knox-Johnson became the first person to sail around the world without stopping.**
It took him 313 days.

Yeah, that's pretty "Great." **The Great Pyramid in Egypt took 100,000 workers and 20 years to construct.** It's made from an estimated 2.3 million limestone blocks.

It's not a stretch!

The Great Wall of China is over 13,000 miles long.
If it were stretched out in a straight line, it would reach
from the North Pole to the South Pole.

**The first known zoo was built in China in approximately
1900 B.C.** It was called the Park of Intelligence.
What a smart idea!

Taking it to the streets!
Concrete has been around since ancient Roman times.
They made it out of lime, water, and volcanic ash.

Don't topple the tower!
**The Eiffel Tower is one of the most famous buildings
in the world, but it was almost demolished in 1909.**
In the end, the French government decided it could be used
as a radio tower and kept it around.

This one is golden.
**Only about 165,000 tons of gold have been mined
from the earth in recorded history.** Put all together,
it would form a cube of only 20 cubic meters.

Czar Nicholas II ruled over Russia from 1894 to 1917. At one point, **Nicholas wanted to build an electric fence around the entire country**. *What a "powerful" idea.*

In 1453, Greek forces in the city of Constantinople fell to the Turkish army. It was a Tuesday, and ever since, **Tuesdays are considered unlucky in Greece**. *Mondays aren't so great either.*

Watch those apples...
In Ancient Greece, throwing an apple to a woman was considered a marriage proposal. If the woman caught the apple, she accepted.

Twice the presents?

Queen Elizabeth II of England has two birthdays.
She celebrates her real one privately on April 21. Then she
has an "official" one that's celebrated with a parade in
June, because April in England is too cold for a parade.

Queen Berengaria ruled England in the 1890s.
Yet she never lived in or even visited England,
preferring to stay in what is today France.
Moving is such a bother.

In 18th-century Paris, street vendors sold baths.
They'd carry tubs and water into people's homes.
And then they'd make a clean break!

**King Alfonso of Spain was deaf, so he employed
a guy to nudge him when the national anthem
was playing.** That way, he knew when to salute.
Here's to you, King Alfonso, for thinking outside the box!

**The legendary composer Ludwig van Beethoven
lost his hearing when he was 45, but he kept
writing music.** He'd clench a stick in his teeth and
hold it against his piano's keyboard, enabling him
to make out faint sounds and vibrations.
Art finds a way.

He's got the skills that pay the bills.
Leonardo da Vinci was a painter, scientist,
mathematician, architect, and writer. But the talent
of which da Vinci was most proud: He could bend
iron with his bare hands.

Probably Leonardo da Vinci's most famous work
was his painting the *Mona Lisa*. **In Italian,
the *Mona Lisa*'s real name is *La Gioconda*,**
which means "joyous woman."
Guess she wasn't the big smiley type.

He was on a first-name basis with the entire world.
Another famous Italian Renaissance artist was
Michelangelo. **His full name was Michelangelo
di Lodovico Buonarroti Simoni.**

Cable news network CNN (it stands for Cable News Network) was founded in 1980. **One of CNN's creators was named William Headline**.

Well, that's the name of the game.

The word *berserk* comes from Berserkers—Viking warriors who dressed in bearskins and howled during battle like they were wild animals.

Berserk indeed!

Kids . . . in . . . space!

The dwarf planet Pluto was discovered in 1930 by astronomer Clyde Tombaugh. **Naming it "Pluto" was the suggestion of 11-year-old Venetia Burney**.

Snow Kidding! On February 18, 1979, it snowed in the Sahara Desert. But it only lasted for about half an hour.

Was it a triple-dog dare?
In 1859, daredevil Charles Blondin became the **first to walk across Niagara Falls on a tightrope**. The walk was technically 160 feet above the Niagara gorge, just down river from the Falls, so some say it didn't count until Nik Wallenda tightrope-walked directly over Niagara Falls, not downstream from it, in 2012.

The winter of 1848 was especially cold in the northeastern United States. **It was so cold that Niagara Falls briefly froze over, with no flowing water**.
Okay, that is pretty cold.

Moving day?
As the result of a February 2010 earthquake, **the city of Concepcion, Chile, shifted 10 feet west**.

Delicious but deadly!
On January 15, 1919, **Boston was hit by a sticky tidal wave** when a 50-foot-tall tank holding 2.3 million gallons of molasses burst. The flood waters rose as high as 25 feet, killing 21 people and injuring 150 more. Cleanup lasted for weeks.

Alexander Graham Bell invented the telephone.
But he never telephoned his wife or mother because they were both hearing-impaired.

Philip Griebel was a German potter. In the 1800s, he invented the garden gnome. Gnome is where the heart is.

You look familiar.
In medieval times, people didn't travel much out of their hometown. **The average person met about 100 other people in their entire life.**

Sorry, Columbus.
The first European explorer to visit North America was Leif Eriksson. He was a Viking, and he came to the New World in about 1000 A.D.

The U.S. bought Alaska from Russia in 1867.
It cost only two cents an acre.
What a deal!

Down Under and through the woods . . .
**Native Australians didn't have maps, but they mapped
out the entire continent.** They wrote and memorized
songs about landmarks, including rocks, trees, and rivers.

This fact rules!
**The only country left on earth that still calls
itself an empire is Japan.** Its current emperor,
the 125th in its history, is named Akihito.

The British Empire was the largest empire of all time.
By 1922, it covered a fifth of the world's land.
Which is a lot of land.

**The first country to give women the right to vote:
New Zealand, in 1893.** Switzerland didn't let women
vote until 1971.
Sheesh, Switzerland!

Get out the vote!
The U.S. didn't officially give women voting rights until 1920, but some women in colonial times voted. **The first woman to vote in North America was Lydia Chapin Taft.** In 1756, she cast a ballot in a Massachusetts Colony election.

The first female elected prime minister: Sirimavo Bandaranaike of Sri Lanka. She first served from 1960 to 1965.

The first of many!

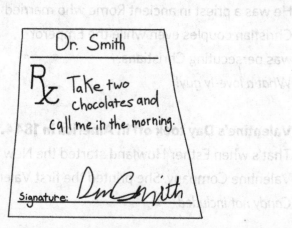

Dr. Smith

Rx Take two chocolates and call me in the morning.

Signature: Dr. Smith

Why is chocolate associated with Valentine's Day? In the 1800s, doctors prescribed chocolate to people who were heartbroken, promising it would soothe their pain. Well, it certainly couldn't hurt.

Be mine!

Heart-shaped boxes of chocolates are the bestselling Valentine's Day candy. About 35 million boxes are sold each February.

Write this down (on a piece of candy).
Conversation Hearts, those chalky little candies
with short messages on them, are made by the company
that makes Necco Wafers. **It produces about
eight billion of them, and it takes 11 months to make
them all.**

Valentine's Day is named after St. Valentine.
He was a priest in ancient Rome who married
Christian couples even while the Emperor
was persecuting Christians.
What a love-ly guy!

Valentine's Day took off in America in 1844.
That's when Esther Howland started the New England
Valentine Company. She printed the first Valentine cards.
Candy not included.

The things we do for love.
**Women in medieval Europe would pin four leaves
to their pillow on the eve of Valentine's Day.
Then they'd eat four hardboiled eggs**—including
the shells. It was said that these steps would
make them dream about their future husband.

In the 18th century, British children went door-to-door on Valentine's Day. They'd sing love songs and beg for cake.

It's never a bad time for cake.

Rice? Who needs rice?
At weddings in medieval England, the guests threw shoes at the bride and groom.

Too much of a winter wonderland?
The least popular month for weddings in the U.S. is January.
Less than 5 percent of couples "tie the knot" then.

Don't even try unless it's February 14th.
Weddings are not permitted at the Empire State Building.
Ever. Well, **except on Valentine's Day.**

The oldest Valentine in existence was sent in 1415 by France's Duke of Orleans. After being put in prison in the Tower of London after a battle, he sent a love letter to his wife. It read: "I am already sick of love, my very gentle valentine, since for me you were born too soon, and I for you was born too late."
What a smooth talker.

Have a heart!
Red is the color of Valentine's Day because it's the color of the heart and blood. For centuries, people thought feelings of love and romance came from the heart.

In some parts of Europe in medieval times, wedding receptions took place in baths. Guests stood in water while small toy boats carried food.
Full speed ahead, veggie tray!

Happy birthday to . . . not you.
In about 3000 B.C., the ancient Egyptians invented the idea of celebrating birthdays. But only those of the queen and male royal family members were celebrated.

In ancient Greece, the birthdays of all adult males were celebrated. Women's and children's birthdays were not observed.
Pass the party hat to your dad, please.

The odds that you, a parent, and a grandparent will all have the same birthday? Very low—about 1 in 160,000.
Happy birthday, happy birthday, happy birthday!

Happy Hedgehog Day!
Groundhog Day is based on an old German holiday called Candlemas, except that they used a hedgehog. When German settlers came to the U.S., they brought the holiday but went with groundhogs, which were more plentiful.

They had wedding cakes in ancient Rome. Guests wished the bride good luck by smashing the cake over her head. Why would they do that to a perfectly good cake?

Sounds pretty fishy... The French call April 1 *Poisson d'Avril*, or "April Fish." French children sometimes prank their friends by taping a picture of a fish onto their back.

St. Patrick's Day as it's celebrated today began in the United States in the late 19th and early 20th centuries.
Large numbers of newly arrived Irish immigrants set the day aside to celebrate their heritage and their homeland.
How lucky for us!

What day is it?!
Some say **April Fools' Day started in the 1500s with a calendar switch**—from the Julian calendar (with the new year starting in March) to the Gregorian calendar (which starts on January 1). People were made fun of if they didn't know about the switch and followed the old calendar.

Couldn't you just dye?
The most popular color to dye eggs is blue.
After that come purple, and then pink.

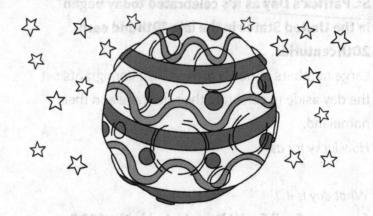

We're over the moon! Why does Easter take place on a different day every year? It's set for the first Sunday after the first full moon of the spring. The earliest that can happen is March 22, and the latest is April 25.

A little cherry in your eggs?

Egg-dying has been an Easter activity since long before artificial dyes were invented. Among the natural dyes used: cherry juice for red eggs, carrots for yellow ones, and red onion skins for purple.

Watch it!
About 87 percent of American parents fill Easter baskets for their kids. Then 81 percent of those parents proceed to steal candy out of them.

Americans didn't know about the Easter Bunny until the late 1600s. Dutch immigrants who settled in Pennsylvania brought the idea to the New World.
Thank you very Dutch!

Ain't no bunny!
In Switzerland, they don't have an Easter Bunny making deliveries. They have an **Easter Cuckoo.**

King of the Easter Bunnies?
In 1307, King Edward I of England asked his kitchen staff **to boil 450 eggs. Then he had them covered in gold leaf** and gave them all away to his servants.

How egg-citing!
In Haux, France, they follow Easter Sunday with Easter Monday. They cook a **gigantic omelette for 1,000 people—** made with about 5,000 eggs.

Kids love getting Easter baskets filled with treat-stuffed plastic eggs. For a kid named Kyle Johnson, the eggs are enough. In 2012, **he set a world record by holding 14 plastic eggs in one hand.**
Eggs-cellent!

On Easter Monday in Hungary, some people engage in a tradition called "sprinkling." Guys dump a bucket of water on a girl they like and ask them for a kiss. They probably won't get one if they do something like that!

They should have a statewide Easter egg hunt!

In Spain, Easter is often called the Feast of Flowers, or *Pascua Florida*. When Spanish explorer Juan Ponce de Leon "discovered" a part of North America on Easter Sunday 1512, **he named the land Florida.**

In 2007, at Cypress Gardens Adventure Park in Winter Haven, Florida, **the biggest Easter egg hunt in history** took place. Almost 10,000 kids searched for 501,000 eggs.

And you just know they found every last one of them.

According to a legend in Finland, Easter is when witches roam the earth. So kids there have fun with it—they smear dirt on their faces, wrap scarves around their heads, and carry brooms.
Sounds more like Halloween than Easter!

Ann Jarvis was a Civil War nurse who helped heal the nation after that conflict by encouraging people to reach out to their mothers with **Mother's Friendship Day**. When she died in 1905, her daughter, Anna Jarvis, received hundreds of cards from people whose lives were touched by her mother, so she started celebrating it in 1908 in West Virginia. **Mother's Day became a national holiday in 1914.**
And the number of cards multiplied!

Dad fact!
Father's Day started as a local holiday in Spokane, Washington, in 1910. It spread around the country but didn't become a permanent national holiday until Richard Nixon signed a bill in 1972.

Say uncle! Say uncle!
You've heard of Mother's Day, and Father's Day, and Grandparents' Day, but did you know **the last Friday of July is Aunt and Uncle's Day?**

Why is Flag Day a thing? June 14 commemorates the day in 1777 that the "stars and stripes" was officially adopted as a symbol of the U.S.A. by the Second Continental Congress.
It was a banner day!

There was a fourth of July before then, but it wasn't the "Fourth of July" until 1781. That's when **Massachusetts became the first state to make Independence Day a holiday.** It became a nationally observed one in 1870.
Did a nationwide cookout break out?!

There are thousands of fireworks displays across the country on the Fourth of July. **The biggest: Macy's Fourth of July Fireworks Show in New York City.** The celebration includes 400,000 rockets launched at a rate of 1,000 per second from six floating barges.
BOOM!

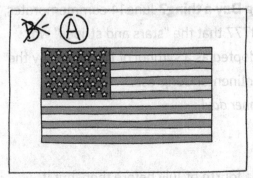

When Alaska and Hawaii became the 49th and 50th states in 1959, a nationwide contest was held to design a new flag – the field of stars had to be updated. The winner: Robert Heft, who came up with his idea as a school project. His teacher gave him a B-minus, but when his design was selected as the winner, the grade was changed to an A. Extra credit?

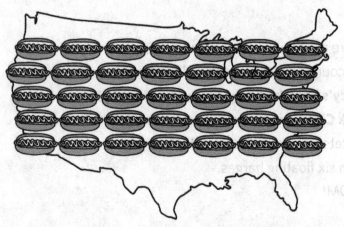

At cookouts across the country, Americans eat a total of 150 million hot dogs every Fourth of July. That's enough to stretch from coast to coast five times over!

Know any good ones?

The only month without a major holiday: August.

However, August 16 is National Tell a Joke Day.

Halloween by any other name . . .

In England, **jack o' lanterns are sometimes called spunkies.**

Spooktacular!

In parts of Iowa, **kids knock on doors on Halloween** but they don't say "trick or treat." **They say "tricks for treats."** Before they get a piece of candy, they have to tell a silly joke.

Ready to visit the turnip patch?
Carving jack o' lanterns came to America with immigrants from Great Britain. Pumpkins are used, because they're a very common vegetable in the U.S. They weren't common in the British Isles, where they used turnips and beets.

A lot of Halloween traditions come from an ancient Irish holiday called Samhain (pronounced "sow-wen"). One Irish Halloween activity: snap-apple. An apple is tied to a doorframe with string and kids try to bite it. *It's like bobbing for apples while standing up!*

One Samhain tradition that stayed in Ireland: **barmback.** It's a fruitcake stuffed with wrapped trinkets that "predict your future" for the months ahead. **If you get a ring in your piece, it means you'll find love. A coin means you'll get rich.**
And at any rate, you get cake!

Trick or treat, smell my feet . . .
November 11 is St. Martin's Day in Belgium and the Netherlands. **Kids celebrate by making paper lanterns and knocking on doors in search of candy.** But instead of saying "trick or treat," they recite poems.

The first Macy's Thanksgiving Day Parade was held in New York City in 1924. There were no giant balloons quite yet, but it did feature a lot of animals from the Central Park Zoo.
And for that, we're thankful.

The first big balloon was introduced into the Macy's Thanksgiving Day Parade in 1927. It was the cartoon character Felix the Cat. *Purrrrrfect!*

No giant balloons were allowed in the Macy's Thanksgiving Day Parade in 1928, 1929, or 1930. Why not? During its first parade in 1927, the Felix balloon got caught in telephone wires . . . and burst into flames. *Not so hot.*

The biggest pumpkin ever: it was 2,624.6 pounds, grown by Mathias Willemijns of Belgium. That's as big as a car!

Not even Superman could save the day.
The 1986 Macy's Thanksgiving Day Parade was a disaster. It was so windy that one balloon knocked over a lamppost, another had its arm ripped off, and a tree ripped off the Superman balloon's hand.

You are getting very sleepy...Some people call that sleepy, extra-full feeling after Thanksgiving dinner a "food coma." The scientific name for it is *postprandial somnolence.*

Be sure to save room for pumpkin pie!
Americans eat a total of 10 million *tons* of turkey each and every Thanksgiving.

Thanksgiving used to be held one week later.
In 1939, President Franklin D. Roosevelt moved it
up a week. That way the Christmas shopping season
could get off to an earlier start.
Happy holidays!

**To purchase all of the birds used in
"The 12 Days of Christmas,"** it would
cost you about $1.3 million.
That's a lot of turtledoves.

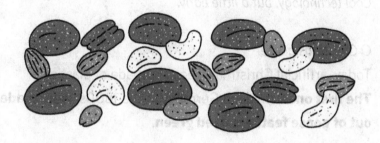

Ever hear about "sugarplums" in old Christmas stories?
What is a sugarplum, anyway? It's chopped dried fruit,
nuts, and spices rolled into a ball
and covered with sugar.

Did someone say cake?

Fruitcake is a classic holiday treat. Most of them are made in Claxton, Georgia, the "fruitcake capital of the world."

Bakeries there make 4 million pounds of fruitcake every year.

Now that's a Christmas gift!

Author Robert Louis Stevenson (who wrote *Treasure Island*) **left his November birthday in his will** to a friend who had been born on Christmas and didn't like it.

The first-ever text message was sent on December 3, 1990. The message said, "Merry Christmas!" *Cool technology, but a little early.*

O Christmas goose!

Today, artificial Christmas trees are made of plastic. **The first ones**, made in Germany in the 1800s, **were made out of goose feathers dyed green**.

Are Santa's reindeer male or female? They are often portrayed as having antlers. Because male reindeer shed their antlers in early December and females have thin antlers through the winter, that means Santa's reindeers are all ladies. *Girl squad!*

Not so minty fresh.
Among the weirder flavors of candy canes available
during the holidays: gravy, bacon, hot sauce, and pickle.

In "The 12 Days of Christmas" song, one of the gifts
is a turtledove. It gets its name from the Latin word
turtur, or dove. That means they're actually called
dove-doves. Wait, can you repeat that?!

Who put on the tree topper?!
According to *Guinness World Records,* **the tallest Christmas
tree of all time was a 221-foot Douglas fir.** It went on
display in 1950 at the Northgate Shopping Center in
Seattle.

Christmas trees are teenagers!

How long does it take to grow a Christmas tree?

The average one sold is about 15 years old.

Not just for Halloween. In Poland, spider webs are a Christmas tree decoration. Spiders are a symbol of goodness and wealth there.

A lot of American kids, and especially kids in Europe, **always get an orange or a tangerine in their Christmas stocking**. That tradition comes from **nuns in the 12th century who left a sock full of nuts and fruit** at the homes of the less fortunate.

We assume the socks weren't used.

Christmas surprise.
According to a central European folk tale, **children who are born on Christmas will grow up to become either lawyers or criminals.**

It wasn't always a holiday?
The first state to officially make Christmas a holiday was Alabama, in 1836. It wasn't a national holiday until 1870.

Mistletoe—the plant that calls for a kiss when you're standing under it with someone—**gets its name from the Old English word *misteltan*, which means "little dung twig."** The plant's seeds are spread by birds that eat the plant and then leave their waste . . . with the seeds still in it.
How romantic!

No tree shall stand!

President Teddy Roosevelt was an environmentalist who wanted to protect nature. For that reason, **he wouldn't allow a Christmas tree in the White House.**

Legos have been one of the most popular toys in the world for more than 40 years. **During the holiday shopping season, 28 sets of Legos are sold every second.** *That's really building something.*

In France, Santa Claus is called Père Noël, or "Father Christmas." Kids set out their shoes and leave cookies for him and carrots for the reindeer. Père Noël returns the favor by filling the shoes with candy. Mmm, shoe candy!

If the 1970 TV special *Santa Claus Is Coming to Town* were to be believed, **Mrs. Claus's first name is Jessica.** *So it's not "Mrs."?*

Just hanging around . . .
In medieval times, actors would perform Christmas plays about Adam and Eve and would hang apples on trees. **That brought about the idea of decorating a tree at Christmas.**

On Christmas in Japan, it's traditional to eat Kentucky Fried Chicken. Families reserve a table and make their orders months in advance. *What are you, chicken?*

When NASA launched the *Voyager* space probe in 1977, engineers made sure they set the spacecraft's trajectory **to avoid any potential collisions with Santa's sleigh** at Christmas.
Thanks, NASA!

Ho! ho! ho!
The Christmas carol "Up on the Housetop" was written in 1864. It mentions "Old St. Nick" delivering presents, making it **the first Christmas song to mention Santa Claus.**

Always get a second opinion.
Songwriters Jay Livingston and Ray Evans called their Christmas song "Tinkle Bell," until Livingston's wife pointed out that most people associate the word "tinkle" with going to the bathroom.

That's when they changed it to "Silver Bells."

Because it's in the Southern Hemisphere, Australian seasons are opposite to North America's. That means Christmas falls right in the middle of summer. Kids don't leave out milk and cookies Down Under-they leave Santa a glass of lemonade. Still enough sugar to fuel his travels!

Where it's Christmas every day!

There are more than **140 towns and cities in the United States with "Christmas" in their names.**

Christmas trees originated in Germany. They were introduced to the United States when German troops came to assist the colonists in the Revolutionary War in the late 1700s.

Danke schön! (That means "Thank you" in German.)

During Christmas in the Canadian province of Newfoundland, **people called Mummers dress up in costumes. Then they go from house to house dancing**, playing music, and trying to get people to guess their true identities.

The great Christmas mystery!

In 1917, **a boat full of explosives blew up in the docks of the city of Halifax, Nova Scotia, Canada.** The city of Boston sent so many people and supplies that as a thank-you, **the Nova Scotia government still sends Boston its official Christmas tree every year.**

That's what the holidays are all about.

Sounds like it would go better with a certain October holiday.
In the 1800s, **it was a Christmas Eve tradition in the U.S. and England to tell ghost stories**.

X marks the holiday.
Why is Christmas abbreviated to Xmas?
X is the Greek letter *chi*, which in Greek is also an abbreviation for "Christ." X + mas = Christmas.

Tough or easy spelling test?
There are at least 16 ways to spell Hanukkah that are technically correct. Because Hanukkah is transliterated from Hebrew letters, there is not an obvious English spelling. The most common are "Hanukkah" and "Chanukah."

That's lit!
The running of the torch isn't reserved for just the Olympics. During Hanukkah in Israel, runners race a burning torch about 20 miles from the Israeli city of Modiin to Jerusalem. The chief rabbi then lights a giant menorah at the Western Wall. Other Jewish communities around the world have joined in similar celebrations.

Our heads are spinning . . .

Major League Dreidel is a real thing. It's a New York City–based association of hard-core dreidel players. Hundreds of people take part in their tournament each year.

Feels like Fryday . . .

Why are fried foods so popular during Hanukkah? Oil is celebrated to remember the miracle of the one day's worth of lamp oil that lasted for eight days.

Say cheese!

The fried-potato pancakes called latkes that are a popular food during Hanukkah didn't start as potatoes. They only became part of the recipe as potatoes became common and less expensive than cheese, which latkes were made from earlier.

A delicious wonder of the world:

On the first night of Hanukkah in 1997, **a 12-foot-high pyramid of 6,400 jelly doughnuts** (traditional treats called "soufganiyot") was built near the Israeli town of Afula.

52 years young!
Founded in 1966, Kwanzaa is a celebration of African
community, family, and culture that begins December 26
and lasts for seven days.

Five, four, three, two, one . . . Happy New Year!
Each New Year's Eve, **a giant ball drops in
New York's Times Square** to ring in the new year.
That ball is called the Star of Hope.

A New Year's Eve tradition in South America:
wearing brightly colored underwear. Legend holds
that if you want to get rich in the new year,
you should wear yellow ones. If you're looking
for love, wear red ones. Hey, why not both?

It's a New Year's Eve tradition in the Philippines for kids to jump up and down 12 times at midnight. Old folk wisdom says it will increase their chances of getting taller in the new year.

Heavy metal!

On New Year's Eve in Germany and Finland, people predict the future by melting lead. They pour hot, liquid lead into water, where it solidifies into a shape. If a heart or ring forms, the person will get married in the new year. If the lead clump looks like a pig, it means you'll never be hungry.

23
ODDBALLS—Random Junk, Quirky Things, Weird Stuff, etc.

Everything has a musical pitch to it. Most toilets flush in the key of E flat. Is it music to your ears?

Flushed away!

In 2014, **38 million gallons of water had to be drained from a reservoir in Portland.** Why?

Somebody went to the bathroom in it!

Right now there are about $40 billion worth of American coins in circulation. Start searching the sofa to collect 'em all!

It pays to save!

The average home has about six pounds of pennies in it. That's not even counting all the dimes, nickels, and quarters.

It's 50-50 odds whether a coin lands on "heads" or "tails," right? Not always. **A penny is more likely to land on heads,** because Lincoln's face weighs more than the Lincoln Memorial on the back.
So maybe call "heads" the next time you have to do a coin toss.

Worth it?

How much does it cost to mint a nickel?

About 10 cents.

Reed all about it!

A dime has exactly 118 ridges around its edge. They're called "reeds."

Big money.

In 2007 Canada issued a $1 million coin.

It weighed 220 pounds and was made of solid gold.

There is an estimated $44 billion worth of unused gift cards floating around out there. More sofa searching?

Half of all bank robberies take place on Friday.
Talk about payday.

U.S. money isn't made from paper. It's made from a blend
of cotton and linen.
Which is why a bill doesn't get destroyed in the wash
when you leave it in your pocket.

Here's a gore-y fact:
The part of a sock where the toes go is called the "toe,"
but the heel has a name, too: the gore.

We found the one good thing about Mondays!
**It's the only day of the week that has a one-word
anagram.** It's "dynamo."

The average office worker types on a computer keyboard an average **of 90,000 keystrokes a day.** *That's a lot of clickety-clacks!*

(Laser) tag, you're it!
The beam in a laser pointer is a low-powered beam of pure light. It could **potentially be seen up to a quarter of a mile away.**

Leather shoes tend to squeak. Athletic shoes don't—which is why they are also called *sneakers.* As quiet as a mouse!

The tallest volcano on Mars is called Olympus Mons. It's about 16 miles tall, about four times as tall as Earth's tallest volcano, South America's Ojos del Salado. It's "only" four miles tall.

The thing that writes in a pencil isn't lead—it's graphite. But there's enough of it in a single pencil to draw a line that's 38 miles long. And you can always erase it if you make a mistake.

TV satellites orbit around the Earth very high in the sky. They operate best at about 22,300 miles above the surface. So then all TV comes...from space?

Waving the white flag.

In 1969, **astronauts left an American flag on the moon**. Scientists say that space radiation **has probably bleached it by now**.

It's not as hot as it could be.

The sun's atmosphere stretches millions of miles into space, past the Earth. **That means that, technically, we live on the sun!**

The sun is bigger than the Earth, but how much bigger? **About a million times bigger.**

Give or take.

Venus rotates in the opposite direction than Earth does, which means sunrises and sunsets work the opposite way there. The sun rises in the west, and it sets in the east.

Only two planets in the solar system don't have any moons: Mercury and Venus. Guess you can't blame crazy behavior on a full moon there.

Things are heating up!

Today, the sun is 30 percent hotter than it was 4.6 billion years ago. (That's when the solar system formed.)

A summer on the planet Uranus lasts more than 20 years.

But hey, so does a winter!

Wake up!

In space no one can hear you snore. That's because **it's impossible to snore in the weightlessness of space.**

But weight!

The earth weighs more every year.

It's put on about 100,000 tons since last year.

The word astronaut comes from two Greek words put together. It literally translates to "star sailor." Come sail away!

Best to just stay on the edges: There's a black hole in the center of the Milky Way galaxy, and it's 14 million miles wide.

Up, up, and away! They look so fluffy, but they're not.
The average cloud weighs more than a million pounds.

If you were able to locate and then cut into **a large enough hailstone, you'd see that it's made up of rings,** just like an onion.
But it won't make your eyes tear up.

How are bolts of lightning like fingerprints?
No two are identical.
They're one of a kind!

Park ranger Roy Sullivan appeared in Guinness World Records **for being struck by lightning more** times than any other person: seven.
We're shocked . . . but not as much as poor Roy.

Air it is!
Snow is only about 10 percent water.
Which means it's about 90 percent air.

All that heat must pack a punch.
Hot water is slightly heavier than cold water.

Ice isn't actually slippery. When pressure is applied to it, a very thin layer melts into cold water.
And that's what is slippery.

Only in the movies...
The chances of sinking in quicksand are slim.
Most quicksand is just a few inches deep.

Outta my way!
At room temperature, an air molecule runs into
a billion other air molecules every second.

True or false: **Mythomaniacs are people who can't stop lying**.
It's true!

You've "almost" got it!
What's the longest word in the English language with all of the letters in alphabetical order? It's *almost*.

3,000,000,000,000,00
0,000,000,00 0,000,00
0,000,000,000

What's a duodecillion?
It's a number: 1 followed by 39 zeroes.
Start counting…

There are a lot of ups and downs.
Research shows that people start to get restless and fidgety if an elevator doesn't come within 40 seconds.

Where did the time go?
Experts say we spend about one year of our lives **looking for lost objects**.

Ahhhh! Tests!
Do you have *scholionophobia?*
That's the technical name for "fear of school."

Feel it!

What's the longest word in the English language that doesn't have a vowel? Rhythm.

We thought we dreamt this up.

There's only one word in English that ends with "mt."
It's "dreamt."

#Trivia.

The "hash" symbol in hashtags has a name.
It's an octotroph.

To lemniscate and beyond!

That curvy infinity sign also has a name.
It's called a lemniscate.

A common diagnosis:
A song that gets stuck in your head is called an earworm. Researchers say at least 90 percent of people get a tune stuck in their head once a week.

Singing is good for you. Taking the mic for one song burns about two calories. Sing your heart out!

Here's a tittle fact . . .

The dot over the letters "i" and "j" is called a tittle.

It's not just orange.

There are a handful of words in English that don't rhyme with anything: orange (of course), purple, silver, and month.

XYZ or YKK?

The YKK on your zipper stands for Yoshida Kogyo Kabushikigaisha. The YKK Group is a Japanese group of manufacturing companies and the world's largest zipper manufacturer.

In 1797, James Hetherington invented the top hat. When he wore it in public, he was arrested for causing a scene. Hats off!

Shiny and similar.

Sapphires are blue and rubies are red.
That's the only difference between those
precious gems—**chemically, they're identical.**

Why are schoolhouses traditionally painted red?
In the 1800s, that was the cheapest paint color.
Nobody would trust a polka-dotted school anyway.

A fact that might float your boat:

In the past, **life jackets were filled with sunflower stems.**
Before plastic foam came along, cork, balsa wood, and
kapok (material from a tropical tree) were also used.

The newest letter in the English alphabet is J.

It wasn't adopted until the 1600s.

If there was no J, would be a PB&J just be a PB?

Does the "O" stand for "Old?"

The oldest letter in our alphabet is O.

It dates back to 3000 B.C.

Stand still and look closely.

**The "Don't" in the "Don't Walk" sign
is misspelled**—the apostrophe is missing.

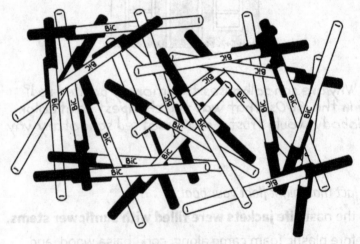

Since 1950, Bic has sold an average of
50 ballpoint pens a second.
That's a lot of writing!

Hello, technical support?

How many photocopier accidents are caused by people sitting on them to make a "copy" of their rear end?
About 25 percent.

Think twice before you hit print!

Which costs more: printer ink or gasoline?
On a gallon-by-gallon basis, the ink costs 1,400 times more than gas.

Say selfie!

Every two minutes, we take more pictures than all of humanity did in the 19th century.

A smartphone is a miracle of modern science. **To make one work requires more than 250,000 individual pieces of patented technology**.
All that to make Twitter work!

Why are phone numbers seven digits long? Because that's about the longest number people can easily memorize. *But then area codes came along to mess it up.*

What is "percussive maintenance"? That's the
technical term for hitting something until it works.
Then you have to try turning it off and back on again.

Bored? Pop the walls of your room!
Engineers Alfred Fielding and Marc Chavannes were actually
working on a **new type of textured wallpaper when they
came up with bubble wrap** in 1957.

But make it snappy.
Want to make rubber bands last longer?
Stick them in the refrigerator.

Do you have a moment?
**In medieval times a "moment" was a measure
of time equal to about 90 seconds.**
Thank you for your time.

You can read this in a jiffy!
A "jiffy" is also an actual, measurable unit of time.
It's one 100th of a second.

Think you can remember this? ***Lethologica* is the inability
to remember a particular word.**
Like, say, lethologica.

The most common street name in the U.S. isn't First Street. It's Second Street.

Huh?

Worms, bears, and gas!

No matter how cold it gets, gasoline won't freeze. When the temperature drops below minus 180°F, it just turns gummy.

Oil is nicknamed "black gold." It can also be red, brown, or green.

But it's always sticky.

That's a big bunny!
All of the dust in your house really adds up.
One home gathers about 40 pounds of dust every year.

Thirsty?

If you poured all the oceans of the world into glasses of water, **there would still be fewer total glasses than there are atoms in just one of those glasses of water.**

He was hoping for a cure but not holding his breath.

Charles Osborne, of Iowa, holds the record for the **longest attack of hiccups—68 years**, from 1922 to 1990. Total estimated hiccups: 430 million.

The largest working yo-yo ever made was more than 10 feet tall and weighed almost 900 pounds. That's about the size of a polar bear. A polar bear can't do as many tricks, though.

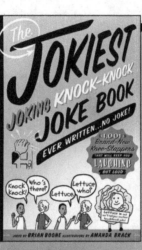

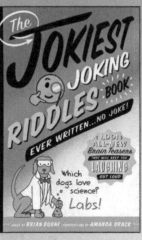